All About AUCTIONS

All About

AUCTIONS

L. G. HEWITT

Illustrations by R. G. Hewitt

CHILTON BOOK COMPANY • *Radnor, Pennsylvania*

Published in Radnor, Pa., by Chilton Book Company
and simultaneously in Don Mills, Ontario, Canada
by Thomas Nelson & Sons, Ltd.
Designed by William E. Lickfield
Manufactured in the United States of America

Library of Congress Cataloging in Publication Data

Hewitt, Linda, 1940-
All about auctions.

Includes index.
1. Auctions. I. Title.
HF5476.H48 1975 658 74-28123
ISBN 0-8019-6160-2
ISBN 0-8019-6161-0 pbk.

For Kay

Acknowledgments

It would be difficult to write a book like this without the active cooperation of many people. So many individuals on both sides of the auction block gave me assistance that it's impossible to distribute proper credit to each, but I again thank all of them.

In all fairness, I must give special thanks for the generous cooperation offered me by retired U.S. Army Major Dennis W. Siebert of the Antique Mart, Mentone, Alabama; and Mr. Donald W. Kichline of Atlanta Auction Galleries, Atlanta, Georgia. To Mr. Kichline, who remains my favorite auctioneer, and to Major Siebert, who operates a country auction of unusual consistency and quality, my sincere gratitude.

It is to the unstinting generosity of these two gentlemen and to all the other auction people who helped me that this book owes much of whatever merit it may possess. Its errors and omissions are entirely my own.

Contents

All About AUCTIONS

Chapter 1

What Is an Auction?

Turn the conversation of any group to auctions, and most people will think of tobacco auctions or perhaps real estate liquidations. Make it clear that you are talking about the kind of auctions where furniture and works of art are sold, and someone will invariably say, "Oh, you mean like Christie's or Sotheby's in London or Parke-Bernet in New York?" If you persist and say that, while these houses are indeed famous for their record breaking sales, what you are really thinking of is the more common variety of auction; most of your listeners will at once assume that you are referring to the homelier sort of country sales.

In practice, today, the auctions that most of us have the opportunity and the means to attend fall somewhere between these extremes; and it is with these auctions that this book is concerned: The auctions where old Minton can follow new Melmac and eighteenth-century English game tables can sit humbly beside 1920s Grand Rapids Jacobean; the auctions where you can spend as much or as little as you like without pushing the national economy off the front page on the one hand or making the auctioneer mad at you on the other.

It's not that the headline-making auctions aren't interesting. They can't help but be. There's something quite fascinating in the idea that anyone has that much money to spend on anything. After all, $415,000 at auction for a 200-year-old French writing desk or $4,800 for a 120-year-old American quilt are not your usual department store price tags. And what about that collected dealer who professed himself to be delighted with his auction purchase of Titian's "Death of Aecton" for a bargain $4 million plus. He'd been, it seems, prepared to break the $5 million plus auction record then held by a Velazquez sold earlier by Christie's.

Don't begin this book thinking that it will aid you at such sales. I have no intention of telling you, for example, how to buy a Modigliani at auction. If you are thinking along those lines, you will have no difficulty finding willing, even eager, assistance. Aid—in the form of expert appraisal, dealers who will bid for you, and reams of readily available research material—is also at hand if you fancy the signed works of an eighteenth-century French *ébéniste* or silver by deLamerie or Mortlake tapestries or Meissen porcelain. This smoothing of the auction path will not be free, of course, but the cost should not bother you unduly.

If, however, your main aim in auctiongoing is to pick up interesting, usable merchandise at a good price, you will be surprised at how few guideposts you will find. Yet intelligent, informed auctiongoing can offer you many advantages. It can, for one thing, stretch the power of your buying dollar. For another, it can enlarge your buying horizons by offering you an everchanging lot of merchandise of almost limitless variety on a regular basis, most of it no longer obtainable in retail stores. Finally, undertaken in the proper spirit, auctiongoing can be fun and oftentimes exciting, as well as profitable. Hopefully, this brief introduction to auctions will help you to achieve the proper spirit with the least amount of tedium.

We'll start this exploration into auctionland by identifying the beast that we are stalking. What is an auction?

What Is an Auction?

Someone who's been stung will tell you. "It's where fools fight to buy junk honest folks would hesitate to give away." An auction addict will protest, "It's like Christmas when you're a kid—look what goodies they've brought us this week." The person who lives with the addict will sigh, "It's where Harry (or Harriet) gets all that stuff we put in the garage."

The more prosaic and less involved dictionary describes it merely as "a public sale at which property or goods are sold to the highest bidder." This definition is precise, yet all-encompassing. By implication there is nothing that can-

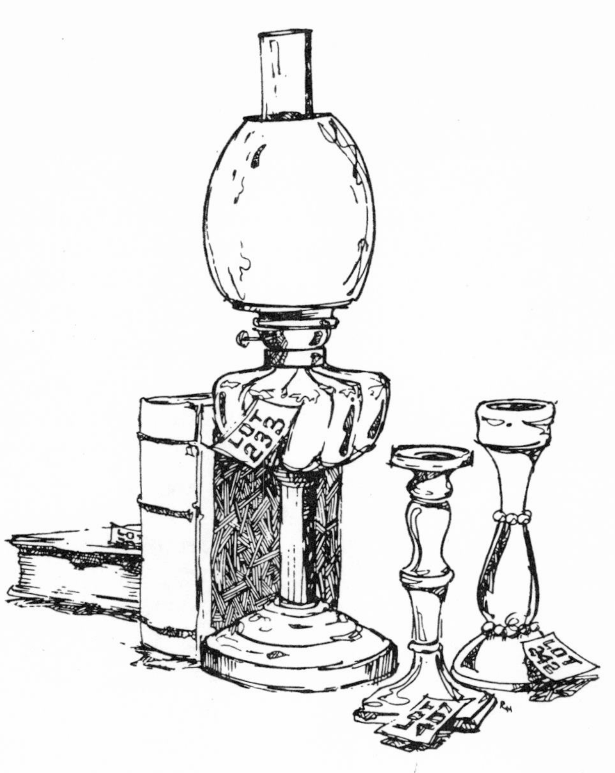

not be sold at auction. In reality, almost everything has indeed stood on the auction block at one time or another, from human beings to abandoned cars to martyrs' bones.

From the beginning of recorded history, man has found the auction a convenient method of disposing of property. The auction has simplified the liquidation of estates, businesses, and collections. It obtains for the seller the highest price that a group of interested and competitive bidders will pay and offers goods to buyers at flexible prices. Basically, then, the auction is an efficient technique for the occasionally necessary or desirable redistribution of goods.

Yet to stop with that description would be like saying that the elephant is a big gray mammal and letting it go at that. The more you go to auctions, the more you will realize that the term leaves room for almost limitless variations. Differences in goods, in auction house policies, in auctioneering styles, and in audience makeup guarantee that almost every auction is distinct from any other in some way. Since covering all of these differences would be impossible in a reasonable space, I have concentrated on certain basic aspects of the auction process and will talk about the general run of auctions. Simply for ease of description in this book, auctions are arbitrarily classified as follows:

Top quality	Majority of the items sell for over $750 each.
High quality	Majority of the items sell for $200–$500 each
Average quality	Majority of the items sell for $25–$125 each.
Garden variety	Majority of the items sell for $2–$25 each.

Most of the specific examples cited deal with auctions in the average category. You will find, as you go to auctions, that these categories are quite arbitrary—that a garden variety auction may produce a surprise treasure that is recognized as such by a couple of sharp bidders and ultimately is sold for hundreds of dollars. You will see items at top quality auctions sell for a few dollars apiece. You will also discover, however, that the basics of the auction remain constant. Whatever the price range, there is merchandise to be sold, and the people who sell it to you rely on the same principles of salesmanship—the primary differences being in the quality of the merchandise and the manner in which the sales principles are exercised.

While admitting that the average auction is as mythical as the unicorn, still we must start somewhere. We will begin at those auctions that offer household goods and art in a price range affordable by Americans of average means.

We will take a look at the kinds of merchandise to be found, the auction houses where you will find it, the men and women who will be selling, and the people who will be sitting in the adjoining seats. In short, we will discuss what to expect at an auction and how to use the auction process to your advantage.

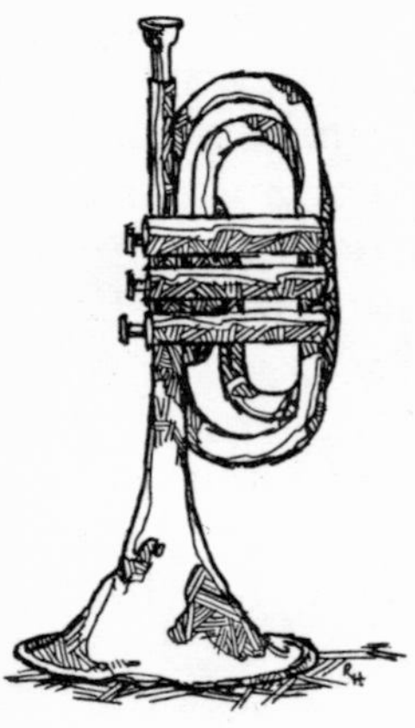

Now, to the blare of rusty trumpets (the auctioneer sold them "as is"), we will pierce the shimmeringly dusty curtain that separates the novice from the auction block. Here, for the first time on any stage—as the old carnival barkers used to say—is the modern American auction, just waiting for your first bid.

Chapter 2

The Goods on the Auction Block

Nestled in the heart of many auctiongoers is the belief that the endless parade of goods appearing on the block has come straight from the elegant abodes of departed souls now enjoying the blissful, but admittedly less well furnished hereafter suite. It is a romantic picture complete with tear stained handkerchiefs and bureau drawers stuffed with treasured photographs and letters. The reminder of man's mortality somehow makes the object on the block more appealing. Also, I suppose, the implication is there that only death could separate the proud owner from these wonderful things.

Not long ago I was sitting behind a sweet-faced woman at a big city auction when a small, taffeta-draped dressing table came up. It was a pretty little thing, although more than a bit the worse for wear, and it was one of those pieces that has managed to retain its distinct personality in spite of its present uncongenial surroundings. Most items on the block look what they are, a chair or a table or a vase, giving no hint of their former use or the people who used them.

But some things—like this little vanity—seem to transmit their particular personal appeal. Perhaps, in this instance, it was the delicate lace that crisscrossed the wilted taffeta skirt or the faded decoration of ribbons and flowers that someone had painstakingly painted on the top. At any rate, when the table was hoisted onto the display stand, the woman in front of me turned to her companion and said tremulously of its former owner: "I wonder what she looked like? I just know she was beautiful, and can't you see her sitting at the vanity, brushing her hair and getting ready to go out? And now she's gone." The last comment was delivered with a gloomy sigh as the next item was brought up.

Now it is quite possible that the vanity's former owner was gone, but her destination was as likely to have been Sao Paulo as Forest Lawn. While it is true that many estates find their way to auction as the result of death, there are also many other forms of impetus. The former owner of the vanity, for example, may simply have been a woman who at last had the opportunity to completely redo her house in her own favorite style. She was probably sitting in the sun somewhere, happily contemplating what the decorators were accomplishing, while we were commiserating over her old furniture.

Things get to auction in a variety of ways. The liquidation of collections—anything from buttons to Brueghels—is a fairly common source of auction goods. Since many collections have considerable intrinsic value, if the collector finds himself in financial difficulty—possibly as a result of his

mania for old Venetian glass—he may be forced to sell the collection. Perhaps more common, a man or a woman who has spent years collecting something, whether it's barbed wire or carnival glass, may suddenly lose interest. Perhaps the collector has simply found a more potent love and has decided to desert barbed wire for insulators, or maybe he has formed such a complete collection that the thrill of discovery no longer exists. Either way, the collection is likely to be liquidated once the initial fascination with the item disappears.

Another reason that collectors return to the auction rooms as consignors is the upgrading of their collections. If a woman collects porcelain, for instance, and her aim is to possess the best possible example of the output of each of the famous porcelain factories of the eighteenth and nineteenth centuries, then at some point she will inevitably acquire a better example. Especially where storage and display are problems, this collector may well choose to have the redundant item or items auctioned.

There are, of course, many ways of disposing of collections in whole or in part. The collector may simply call up other collectors and pass the word about what he is interested in selling. He may call a dealer who specializes in the collectible item or items. He may try to sell to a museum what he no longer wants or, if money is no problem for him, give his extra treasure to the institution, which will ensure him a sort of temporary immortality and frequently a nice savings on his income tax.

But there is no denying that the auction exerts a special attraction for collectors about to clean house. Perhaps it is at least partly financial. If the collection is a good one and the auction house does a competent job of advertising it, interested buyers may come from all over the country and even abroad. That means that the owner will have a large number of potential buyers already interested in the specific item or sort of item that he has collected. Naturally, the competition engendered by this circumstance tends to boost prices both on individual articles and on the collection as a whole.

Take the sale of the collection of folk art assembled by

Pennsylvania farmer Walter Himmelreich, for example. At the Pennypacker Auction Center in the autumn of 1971, the bidding was so brisk that many dealers were forced to drop out of the contest. Hundreds of bidders and potential bidders saw the 446 items in the sale realize almost $109,000, with some individual articles setting new American auction price records.

Apart from financial gain, the auction of his collection gives the collector a memorial of sorts while he still lives. There is, I have been told, something very heady about watching knowledgeable people gather for the express purpose of competing to pay high prices for what one has assembled. Also, the auction catalogue is permanent proof of the collector's accomplishment. I am reminded of the passage in Wesley Towner's fascinating book *The Elegant Auctioneers* describing the appeal of a book auction at the old American Art Association of New York in the 1920s. The AAA made a practice of issuing well written and beautifully illustrated catalogues on important book sales, catalogues that were—as they were intended to be— a tribute to the consignors's "literary discernment," as well as a reminder of an exciting sale and the cash that it produced.

Museums, those collectors on a larger scale, will often consign redundant items to the auction block. Sometimes this is a matter of routine policy; sometimes the product of financial necessity.

Although the auctioning of museum-owned pieces elicits a reaction from many art patrons comparable to that called forth from vampires by a full moon, there is a certain logic to the process. If a museum is trying to achieve a balanced collection, say of paintings representative of the best or at least the more superior artistic offerings of bygone and present times, then it does not need half a dozen Corots. Better to have two Corots and to auction the other four and use the proceeds to buy works by artists or schools not already represented in the museum. The critics of this practice do not deny the truth of the reasoning, but say that the sale of a museum-owned article, assuming it to have been donated in the first place, betrays the intent of the original donor. If the long dead Mrs. Van Smythe–Brown gave that Whistler to the local museum in memory of the departed Mr. Van Smythe–Brown back in 1923, the argument goes, then the museum should hang onto it, no matter what. Otherwise, what guarantee do potential donors have that their own gifts will not someday be disposed of in the same cavalier fashion? There is much to be said for both points of view, but as of now some museums are still consigning to auction articles whose selling price will offset the disadvantage of their loss to the museum.

Museums are not the only corporate entity occasionally guilty of wanting the cash more than the possession. I am thinking, for example, of the Cranbrook Academy's decision to sell over 1,000 works of art in an attempt to raise $2 million for its endowment fund. (Their goal was considerably nearer after the first auction—at Parke-Bernet in New York—when a London dealer paid $260,000 for Henry Moore's "Reclining Figure.")

Some auctions provide a sad footnote to the end of an era in business: the Depression sales and, more recently, the public auction of the memorabilia of the Penn Central. Relics of over one hundred years in the railroad business, deemed superluous to the continued operation of the foundering transportation giant, were sold by Samuel T. Freeman & Company, appropriately enough at the South Concourse of the Penn Central Station in Philadelphia. Other businesses choose to have old office fittings auctioned rather than transport them to a new location when the company moves. Some manufacturing firms dispose of seconds or rejects by auction.

Another source of auction goods is the traditional enemy of the auction house, the antique or gift shop. If a shop is going out of business, then its entire stock of merchandise may end up on the block. If the shop was well known and dealt in high quality goods, then the auction will be well attended and the bidding usually brisk, allowing for a speedy and usually profitable liquidation of the stock.

Dealers who have no thought of liquidation per se also turn to auctions to achieve a faster turnover. Most antique and gift shops are relatively small so that storage and display of merchandise pose considerable problems, and even the most astute buyer occasionally overestimates the appeal of certain items for her clientele. This means that the dealer is faced with the option of setting the consistently unsaleable piece in a dark corner in the event someone should ask for it someday or trying to sell it away from her shop, hopefully for a high enough price to recoup her original investment. If a dealer has good contacts with other dealers, she may be able to make a swap with them, getting rid of her white elephant but often at the cost of taking one of theirs or, if the transaction is for cash, to sell it to another dealer, possibly at a loss.

More and more dealers, particularly in the Atlantic seaboard states, are turning to the auction as a timesaving method of stock turnover. Some even do it on a regular basis so that any piece that has not sold or generated any particular customer interest within a certain period of time may find

itself automatically on its way to auction. Since the people who patronize auctions and the people who haunt shops are not always the same, it is quite possible that even at local auction the dealer may make almost as good a profit as if she had sold the piece in her own shop.

An increasingly important source of auction goods is foreign imports. There are firms in England and Western Europe that specialize in exporting large shipping containers of antiques and near-antiques to the United States. Today many auction houses are being forced to use these firms as their primary source of goods because of the fierce competi-

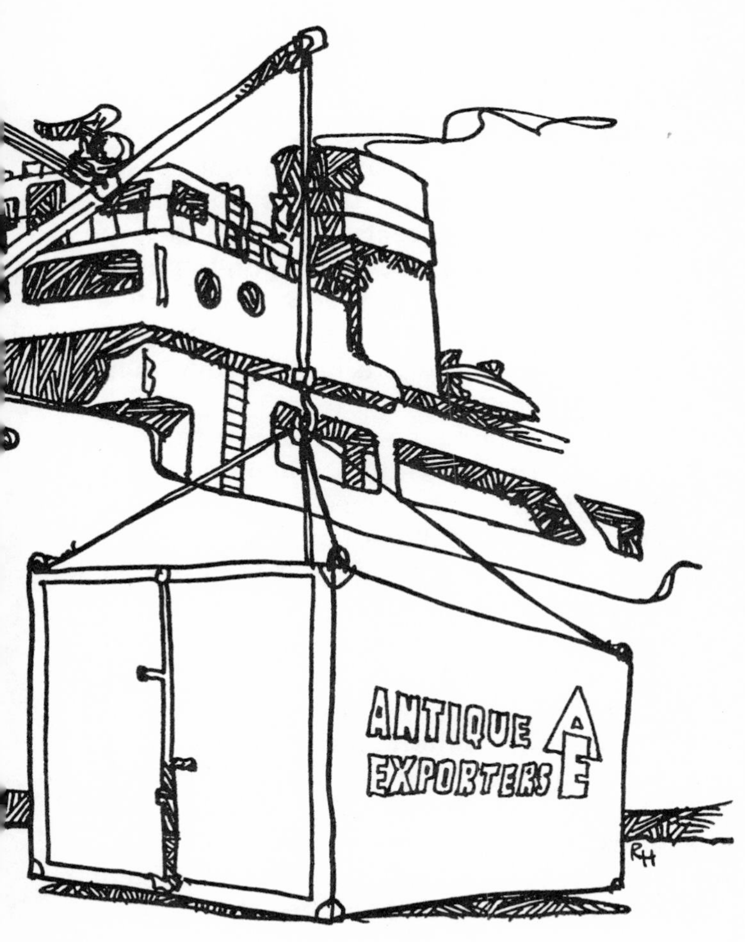

tion for auctionables. The prosperous or adventurous auction house proprietor may himself make the Grand Tour on a regular basis, finding his own sources abroad for merchandise.

Goods are imported not only from abroad, but also from distant parts of the United States by haulers. It is almost a truism in the antique business that what you can barely give away in one area will elicit gasps of astonishment and spirited bidding in another. It was out of this disparity in taste and preference that the practice of hauling antiques about from state to state began. New England was long a prime source in this mostly one-way trade, and castoff Vermont farmhouse furniture, for example, has wended many a weary mile to Georgia and Tennessee and Texas.

And finally we come back to that traditional source of auction goods: the estates of the dead. It has long been customary in some sections of the United States for heirs to choose what they want of the deceased's personal possessions and household goods and send the rest to auction. Sometimes, the deceased's will directs that his estate be auctioned. Even when the will was not specific on the point, a lawyer or bank which has been appointed executor under the will may choose to have all real and personal property auctioned, particularly when there is a hint of squabbling over who shall get what.

And, as we said at the beginning, some estates make their way to auction when no one has died. An older couple moving to an apartment from a large house may send whatever they cannot use in the smaller quarters to auction. Someone who has accumulated a hodge podge of furnishings may decide that he now wants everything Early American. A family moving across country may not wish the trouble and expense of transporting their possessions.

There are many ways for things to get to auction. Now that we've looked briefly at some of them, let's see just exactly what is appearing on the auction block these days. Once you get away from Parke-Bernet in New York and a few other large big-city galleries, an Old Master or a piece of Sèvres porcelain or anything else of high value is unlikely to appear. The reason is simple: Outside of these centers, there are not enough potential bidders willing to spend enormous sums at auction. Not that the big bidders all live in or near New York, for example, but a city like this is a gathering point for serious collectors from all over. Thus, the important items tend to gather there also.

"Big" auctionables aside, what can you expect to find when you walk into an average American auction today? To a large extent, the answer depends on the auction house you are patronizing. There are some houses that specialize in a particular sort of goods, handling nothing but old (that is, pre-World War I) American goods, foreign imports, or estates. Some auction houses are known for their success with a type of sale—such as primitives, glass, art, etc.

Looking over my collection of auction catalogues and my notes on houses that do not furnish catalogues or lists, I am convinced that you may see absolutely anything at auction sooner or later, including some things whose existence you might doubt if the physical proof were not being waved in front of your eyes. Generally speaking, however, auctions and the goods that they present fall into certain categories.

First we'll look at the so-called country auctions. Although this term probably originated as a description of the locale of the auction, it has also come to mean a sale composed mostly of goods brought in from another area by the truck load. There are many variations in quality and quantity included in the country auction designation.

In New England, country auctions are usually made up of consignments from local people. In the South and West, the country auction usually features merchandise hauled in by experienced pickers from New England or the North Central states, along with some consignments from local people.

In the higher quality country auction, which would be an average auction in the terms of this book, the merchandise is usually in fair to good condition. The variety of goods offered ranges from small-to-medium-sized furniture (with an occasional large piece thrown in for audience interest), frames, old prints, silverplate, and the like to old books and magazines. There is not, proportionately, a great deal of porcelain or earthenware, as these items pose packing problems. There are often Victorian or Edwardian Chandeliers. The furniture is usually also Victorian or Edwardian, with some Empire and even 1920s products upon occasion. Old wicker will come up from time to time. Turn-of-the-century wooden office furniture is fairly common. Sometimes there will be old scrapbooks, photo albums, even old phonograph cylinders.

The garden variety country auction, also made up of haulers' pickings and local consignments, specializes in what many in the trade call "junque" (translatable in current jargon as interesting junk). This is possibly the most confusing assortment of goods that you are likely to find in one auction. From old and rusted appliances to almost new lawn mowers, from anything plastic that has been cheaply made to solid but often aesthetically unappealing turn-of-the-century furniture of the less valuable sort. The raspy voiced country auctioneer treats all his wares the same, even the occasional good piece that manages to sneak in—doubtless as a tribute to the law of averages and the unlikelihood of anything being all bad. At a particularly dreary country auction that I recently attended, a beautiful and old child's Windsor rocker in excellent condition was lost in the midst of rusty flatirons, enormous stacks of 78 RPM records, new insulators, wooden rolling pins, "an-

tique'' electric appliances, used tools, beer signs and clocks, cider presses, miscellaneous furniture parts such as bed posts or chair legs, beatup golf clubs, collapsed basketballs, and cracked chamber pots.

The auction houses specializing in foreign imports offer almost as wide a variety of goods as the garden variety auction. As might be expected, the imports are chosen for their potential attractiveness to an audience. Here you will see very little of the flotsam and jetsam of life unless it is appealing flotsam and jetsam. What you will see is a lot of good looking merchandise falling within certain fairly well defined categories. Perhaps the most numerous category consists of smaller decorative items—bowl and pitcher sets, metal or porcelain planters, cruet sets, Staffordshire dogs and figurines, dresser or trinket sets, perfume bottles, oriental vases, and the like. Next in importance must come porcelain, rarely entire sets of dinnerware but miscellaneous cake plates, platters, tureens, and teapots. Glassware is another frequent offering—most often in the form of cut, Bristol, or etched glass, with an occasional piece of art glass. Brass comes up a lot—hammered and rolled into every conceivable shape for a wide range of uses, but most often in the form of wastebaskets, trays, candlesticks, fire tools, coal hods, scuttles, watering cans, and jelly pans. Clocks of every possible size and age are frequent entries in the import-auction stakes.

Many auction imports bear mute testimony to a distant and sometimes vanished way of life. Enormous beer steins of glass, porcelain, or pewter; mustache cups; lap desks; tea caddies; biscuit barrels; samovars; toast forks; oversized tea sets of Victorian or Edwardian silverplate; even stuffed birds sitting on dead branches in glass boxes rarely go begging for bidders. Neither do certain items which fit no distinct category—things like old European grocery scales, German helmets, swords, and musical instruments (with zithers, violins, hunting horns, and pump organs the leaders here).

The fine arts are scantily represented. There are usually quite good eighteenth and nineteenth-century lithographs and engravings of foreign personages—often royalty, military heroes, actors, or reigning beauties—and landscapes that feature vistas of open countryside enhanced by a country house. The few oil paintings that appear tend to be mediocre landscapes or amateur-executed portraits or poor copies of famous works. Watercolors are usually unintentionally watery seascapes. Small bronzes are not uncommon, and at times you will see a veritable flood of the less expensive metal figures.

Comparatively speaking, very little furniture is put up. This is because most patrons come to buy things of a decorative nature, not household furnishings in the strictest sense of the term. The furniture that is sold tends to be in the nature of smaller items that can be used for display: muffin stands, tea and game tables, plant stands, curio cabinets, vitrines, small chests, and of course the ubiquitous chocolate cabinet. Occasionally an unusual item will appear—a Victorian dental cabinet of burled walnut and marble, perhaps, or an Edwardian stereopticon encased in a small cabinet. A recent development has been the flood of old hotel furniture. If you think that inlaid wardrobe looks familiar, it's probably because you hung your clothes in it, or one like it, the year you went to Edinburgh or Baden or Amsterdam.

Generally, the quality of items offered tends to be consistent and relatively good at the better import auctions. Yet the same degree of control and selectivity that ensures this consistency also creates a certain conformity. Most import auctions fall in either the average or the high quality auction category in terms of price.

At auction houses handling mostly estates, the overall quality from sale to sale is not as consistent as at import auction houses. This is understandable, as the latter can more easily control the flow of merchandise into the showroom, while the former is dependent, to some extent, on factors beyond its control. One week the estate specialist may have the lifetime accumulation of a discerning and creative collector on the block; while the next he may have nothing but the almost new, low quality leavings of a family about to move and unwilling to pay moving charges on their worn household articles.

Unlike other sorts of auctions, the estate auction must, almost of necessity, offer the entire spectrum of quantity and quality. Here you can see not only every style and form of furniture (and in every price range), but also every other item that makes an empty house a cluttered home. Complete sets of dinnerware—dishes, silver or silverplated flatware, crystal—and linen come up frequently. Drapes, rugs, even old wall-to-wall carpeting, as well as all sorts of lighting fixtures and mirrors, appear on the block. Any sort of large and small appliances may turn up—stoves, refrigerators, air conditioners, heaters, toasters, mixers, blenders, electric knives, hair dryers, ad infinitum.

Many estate sales include home entertainment equipment such as pianos, organs, television sets, radios, phonographs, tape decks, movie and slide projectors, cameras, and smaller musical instruments. Tennis rackets, footballs, basketball hoops, skis, fishing and hunting equipment, including guns—all sorts of sports articles form part of many estate auctions. A wide array of graphics—from fine oils and hand-cut silhouettes to cliché reproductions in plastic frames, from signed bronzes to dime store figurines—is the norm. Garden statuary, often of overwhelming size and weight, show up from time to time, as do house plants.

Books, jewelry, furs, umbrellas, even cookware and bedding have their turn. In fact, the most personal articles are often sold alongside the impersonal. Old pipes, cigarette holders, family photo albums, scrapbooks, school annuals, hand-written recipe albums, original needlework, and old military medals will occasionally appear on the block. Presentation pieces—anything from tureens to symbolic statuettes, usually silver or brass, commemorating notable occasions like a fiftieth wedding anniversary or the winning of some school or club event—come up with predictable regularity.

A variation of the estate auction is the affair staged by some group, often church or club connected. Sometimes the club hires an auction house to assemble merchandise of a certain kind or quality for a benefit sale. More often and more interestingly, however, these auctions represent the gleanings from the attics of the members and their friends. The end result is an auction that can encompass everything from miscellaneous furniture to needlework. An auction conducted by the Women of St. Mary's Church of Northfield, Vermont, for instance, produced not only the usual assortment of goods, but also a silver cup, saucer and spoon given one Lord and Lady Inchcape as a wedding present by the Maharajah of Kaluhapur. While not every auction of this sort boasts such a novelty, many produce items beyond one's expectation and, sometimes, imagination.

Clearance or, as they are sometimes called, consignment auctions are held by almost every sort of auction house and usually consist of the rag-tag remnants from various sources. Here, anything goes. Much of the merchandise is damaged or so ugly that it cannot possibly sell at regular auction. Here you will see lots of cups without saucers, decanters with chipped lips, damp-spotted linens, faded drapes, torn rugs, cracked paperweights, boxes of furniture parts, books without bindings, and chairs without legs. Occasionally a good (though never great) piece will sneak in, but mostly this is what the term "clearance" implies: the clearing of the dark, dusty corners into which fifth rate or badly damaged merchandise inevitably gets pushed.

Apart from these general kinds of auctions described above, you may encounter auctions featuring only one sort of merchandise. At an auction of primitives, for example, you can forget cut glass of the brilliant period and concentrate on cobbler's benches and wooden kitchen implements, spinning wheels and old iron banks. There are auctions that feature only graphics and sculpture, dolls, children's books, porcelain, or glassware. Some auctions concentrate on a style or a period, like all nineteenth-century or all Pennsylvania Dutch. Best publicized of these specialized auctions were those in California in which some of Hollywood's financially ailing film studios disposed of their surplus movie props. There you could buy a coat worn by Clark Gable or a huge stuffed ape used as scenery in a horror film.

Basically, this description encompasses the different kinds of auctions that you are likely to encounter in much of America. Naturally, there can be overlapping. Houses that specialize in estate auctions also sell imports, while the house that normally handles imports may sell out a local antique shop. Too, the auction is not always what it proclaims itself. In many areas, for instance, country auctions—which imply to many people old or at least used American merchandise—actually import much of their merchandise from abroad.

From even this brief discussion, you can see that it is impossible to say with any degree of accuracy exactly what the auctiongoer will find at any given sale. Quantity and quality of merchandise offered vary not only from auction house to auction house, but also from sale to sale of any given auction house. When you have attended a few auctions, you begin to get a feel for what to expect from the advertising for the auction and also from the house offering the sale.

If you go to enough auctions, you will begin to notice the emergence of certain trends in merchandise; these trends affect what you will find at subsequent auctions. At the moment, there are many people collecting depression glass with an intensity that is truly surprising, considering the low status of this glass just a few years ago when it was given away in movie houses as prizes or used as product premiums. There are a lot of people around who are willing to pay bonanza prices for clocks, almost any kind of clock it seems. Fancy Victorian and Edwardian silver and silverplate have achieved a new popularity. Anything from the Art

Nouveau and Art Deco periods is currently a hot collector's item in almost all areas of the country. You will attend few auctions today, and probably for some time to come, that will not feature at least some items from one or more of the above classifications. Like any sensible business, the auction house offers what the customer wants to buy to the extent that it is able.

As for age, most of the merchandise that you see will not—possibly contrary to your expectations—be antique, but rather old or even new. By American law applied by customs officials when determining duty-free passage of genuine antiques, the term "antique" refers to any item at least 100 years old, which leaves "old" to cover 99 years to yesterday. "New" is obvious, and new merchandise of all kinds comes up more often than you might expect. Sometimes it is obviously new, as when the auctioneer points to a toaster and proudly proclaims, "We took it out of its unopened box. It was bought last year, they tell us, but never used." Sometimes it is meant to look anything but new, as when the auctioneer says hurriedly, "Looks like a fine piece of old carnival glass to me, in good condition."

I have been to several auctions that were dominated by newer, in some instances almost new, merchandise. It is, however, rare to see merchandise that is new in spirit as well as age, with the exception of art objects in the higher to top quality auctions. You won't often see glass and chrome and steel furnishings, for example. Most of the newer stuff, especially furniture, tends to be at least vaguely indebted to older styles, usually Chippendale, Sheraton, Hepplewhite, Queen Anne, Jacobean, and hybridizations of Louis XV and XVI. Furniture appearing at auction today usually originated between the years 1820 and 1940, to use two convenient, admittedly arbitrary dates. It is rare to see much furniture at the average auction that can be proven to have an earlier date, and furniture produced after 1940 rarely appears, either because the quality of much of it is so bad that it would bring next to nothing or because most of it is still in use. Most common style periods in furniture appearing today are late Empire (1820-1840), later Victorian (1875-1900), and Edwardian (1900-1914).

The Goods on the Auction Block

It is inevitable that the goods appearing on the estate auction block reflect the dying off of their original possessors, those people who were forming households during the years 1905 to 1925. For this reason, you will see a lot of the sort of china and furniture and silver that were popular during these years—most notable of which are art nouveau inspired silver, heavily flowered porcelain, and furniture reproductions in the pseudo–Queen Anne style of the 1910s and the mock-Jacobean style of the 1920s.

Import auctions generally feature furniture dating from 1820 to 1910, porcelain from 1820 to 1940, and glassware from the 1880s onward.

More and more, at every sort of auction, you find the so-called new antiques, usually defined as any article made after 1900. Many of these objects—particularly those relating to the early business world of this century—have no intrinsic or aesthetic value, but are simply riding the crest of the nostalgia wave. Still, as older articles suffer the inevitable attrition wrought by time and use, becoming more and more desirable, it is likely that the average auction houses will turn increasingly to the Edwardian era and those decades following it for the bulk of their sales.

Of only one thing can you be sure: no matter what comprises the bulk of auctionables, half the people in any audience will call it junk, while the other half will bid furiously to possess it.

Chapter 3

The Auction House

"A lot of these fellows get their hands on a thousand dollars, rent a hall, buy a bunch of cheap merchandise, hire a hog caller, and call themselves an auction house. There's a lot more to it than that."

There is, indeed, as this experienced auction operator claims, more to it than that. Just how much more, of course, depends on the individual auction house, which is only to be expected in an endeavor that is controlled not only by the exigencies of supply and demand and cost accounting, but also those of show business. Just how much show business and how much cost accounting is the decision made by each auction house. Still, whatever the blend, all auction houses share certain needs and problems.

As might be assumed, the basic problems of the auction house are concerned with merchandise: finding it, arranging for it to be sold, producing a reasonable number of people to bid on it, and persuading the auctiongoers to pay a good price.

Secondary problems include the transportation and display of merchandise, provision of facilities for the sale, maintenance of a staff to handle selling and accounting chores, theft and fraud on the part of customers, malicious whispering campaigns and local laws meant to harass the auction house and eliminate the threat of potential competition that it poses to local antique shops.

The primary function of the auction house is to sell merchandise to bidders. The fulfillment of this function necessitates the utilization of fairly complex business techniques and organization.

The procurement of goods is naturally the first order of business. Auction goods may be either consigned or house-owned.

As we have seen, consigned goods can come from many sources, but they rarely if ever come automatically. It is the job of the auction house to see that goods are consigned to it rather than disposed of in some other way. Trust departments of banks, lawyers acting as executors, heirs of estates, referees in bankruptcy, or any other individual or organization likely to be in a position to dispose of auctionable property must be persuaded to use the auction house's facilities. To this end, advertising and individual solicitation are often used.

Just how goods are brought to auction is a fascinating story in itself. Often the auction house proprietor must use the subtlest diplomacy and shrewdest business ploys to acquire the items that must continuously flow through his establishment. First he must convince the potential consignor that an auction is the logical way to liquidate the saleable items. Then the consignor must be made to feel that this particular auction house will do the best job for him at a fair cost. Convincing the would-be consignor is not always easy. In addition to the eternal rumors concerning the honesty of auction houses in general, the solicitor for the auction house must also counter an ingrained distaste for auctions that exists even today in some parts of the country and in some segments of society. This ingrained distaste is a special problem when it comes to the disposition of estates.

Many times the heirs and executors will resist the idea of

having the estate auctioned, even when this process might bring about a more efficient disposal of the estate. Often, they feel that the deceased would not like having his or her things on the block and that an auction somehow taints the memory of the departed.

This reluctance to consign estates to auction exists all over the country to some extent, but the South has long been notorious for nurturing this attitude. "In the South," according to one noted auctioneer and auction house proprietor, "as recently as a few years ago, an auction was not consid-

ered respectable. It was reminiscent of bankruptcy sales and implied, to many 'nice' people, a lack of feeling on the part of the consignors. That's changing now, but it's been a long, hard chore to convince some of these people."

In a way, even to an auctiongoer, this attitude is understandable; in a way, it is illogical. If the family and heirs do not want all of the estate, the remnant must be disposed of in some way. Unless the family is willing to use it for landfill at the city dump, it must either be sold or donated to some charity. Whichever solution is chosen, it is likely—indeed inevitable—that uncaring strangers are going to paw Aunt Hetty's linens and sit in Cousin Jack's favorite chair. In the final analysis, the only difference lies in the method of selling. Which is more unfeeling: an auction or a second-hand furniture store?

The auction house soliciting estate auctions must be prepared to furnish certain services to the consignors. These services can vary greatly, depending on the sort of auction to

be held. As a rule, they begin with a representative of the auction house inventorying and appraising the material to be auctioned.

Most estate auctions are sold from the premises of the auction house, which must have a hall or auditorium large enough to contain a reasonable number of bidders. Some auction houses operate "under the tent" part of the time, which has the advantage of location flexibility, but which confronts them with the additional problems of transporting the tent, putting it up, and taking it down. Transportation of the merchandise to the auction hall or tent, any cleaning or repairs, cataloguing, and display are the responsibility of the auction house, although charges may be made against the proceeds of the auction to cover some of these expenses.

Sometimes an estate is auctioned from the house it occupies, as at the 1971 Butterfield & Butterfield sale of the contents of Grayhill in Beverly Hills, home of movie actor George Hamilton and his family. Sometimes the auction is on the grounds of the property, as when Christie's sold the remnants of Anna Thomson Dodge's fabulous collection under a large yellow and green striped tent on the front lawn of Rose Terrace, the late Mrs. Dodge's mansion in Grosse Pointe Farms, Michigan. Auctions much humbler than these are sometimes sold from the home of the owner or his heirs if the consignor is willing.

There are definite advantages in selling from the present location of the property to be auctioned. For one thing, transportation of the merchandise is unnecessary. For another, many auctiongoers prefer this sort of sale, finding it more interesting to see the items to be auctioned in their native habitat. Particularly when the house involved is a famous one, sale attendance will probably be unusually good and the bidding brisk. On the other hand, there are also disadvantages. Unless the house was crammed with a wide assortment of furnishings in good condition, the auction house may have to make additions to the sale, that is, to transport merchandise from the auction house to the site of the sale in order to present a well-balanced sale to customers. The auction staff must be transported to the sale. The physical layout of few houses is suited to a large gathering of people in any one spot so that bidding tends to develop into a shouting contest, a sort of room-to-room round robin. If the auctioneer tires of this and moves the sale out of doors, there is always the danger that the weather may turn nasty, driving customers away.

In any event, many consignors are not willing to have sales conducted in their homes or those of their deceased relatives. To their way of thinking, auctioning the merchandise is one thing, having hordes of strangers tramp through the old homestead something else again.

Wherever held, the sale is conducted under the auspices of the auction house, and the house's staff must keep accurate records of who bought what for how much and what remained unsold. The house must also collect the proper amount of money from the buyers and give them what they have bought. There, generally speaking, the auction house's responsibility for the sold merchandise ends. Few auction houses deliver, and many do not provide any long-term or even short-term storage facilities.

Then the house must render full accounts to the consignor, along with monies sufficient to cover the auction proceeds less chargeable expenses and less the house's commission. Most houses specializing in estates charge 15 to 20 percent for the average sale, although commission cutting is not unknown when there is competition for a particular lot. As one well-known house advertises: "Commission subject to negotiation depending on value of consignment."

Merchandise that remains unsold is handled according to whatever agreement the auction house has with the consignor. The house may retain unsold items and try them at another auction, or it may attempt to sell them "over the counter" to collectors or dealers who missed the auction or perhaps failed to bid at the time. The unsold items may be returned to the consignor, which probably happens most frequently in the case of objects with a high intrinsic or sentimental value on which a large reserve was placed—the consignor evidently feeling that he was willing to part with his elephant foot umbrella stand or what have you only if he got enough money to salve the pain of separation. Whatever is done with unsold merchandise, the auction house is usually compensated in some way for its handling of the transaction. One common form of compensation involves the payment to the house by the consignor of a small percentage, say 2½ percent, of either the reserve or the amount of the final bid before the house withdrew the merchandise from the auction.

Individuals or institutions consigning several articles expect much the same sort of service as those consigning a boxcar full of furniture. In fact, the auction house with any pretense to prestige and volume must employ all sorts of employees to handle these different activities so necessary to the successful outcome of the auction sale. Consignors do not lurk around every corner, and in many areas of the country there is at least some competition for any but the most miserable of lots. Therefore, the auction house's reputation for efficiency and fairness is vital.

There are, as we have seen, people who make a business of supplying the auctions with merchandise. These are the pickers or haulers who supply the so-called country auctions and the English and European exporters who service their city cousins.

The pickers will scour a geographical area that has proven a good source of old or interesting things, usually a rural or an economically depressed urban area that people are leaving. Such areas are particularly promising if they at one time enjoyed a period of prosperity so that large houses were built and furnished. In the palmy days of yore, pickers—who were then relatively few in number—could knock on the front door of an interesting house and ask if there were anything for sale, inquiring specifically about the contents of the attic, basement, and any outbuildings. As a rule, their reception was friendly. Now the pickers have become a veritable army of antique-crazed locusts, and occupants of interesting old houses have taken to putting "Posted" signs on their front gates and hiding behind their shutters whenever a stranger appears.

One successful picker gets around the competition by advertising that he will pay one dollar to look in your attic. He boasts that not only has he made many real finds in this way with less effort on his part, but also that he has yet to have anyone ask him for the dollar. Other pickers scour estate sales, junk shops, defunct business sales, dumps, even local auctions for bargains. Bargain, of course, meaning anything that he can haul sometimes hundreds or even thousands of miles and still sell for enough to clear a profit after paying his expenses.

The picker hauls his merchandise to an auction house in an area where it will bring more than in the area of its origin. He usually does this under a formal or informal contract with the auction house, rarely on speculation. The typical agreement calls for the hauler to produce goods of a certain kind on a given date, the auction house to provide a hall in which to hold the sale, an auctioneer, an audience, and a record keeper. For its part, the auction house keeps a commission ranging usually from 10 to 15 percent. The hauler gets the rest. A hauler who has built up a reputation for real finds will attract a following so that auction hounds will go to any sale in the area supplied by him.

Auction houses charging the higher commission may provide helpers to unload the truck, to arrange the merchandise display for pre-auction inspection by customers, and to clean up after the auction is over. For the lower rate of commission, the auction house usually does nothing but provide the premises, sell the goods, keep track of who bought them, and collect the money, expecting the hauler himself to handle loading and unloading, display, and housekeeping.

Although there are obvious advantages to the auction operator in using haulers—mainly little capital investment or risk and the need for relatively few full-time employees—there are also several problems. One operator of a highly successful country auction in northeastern Alabama said that he could go on all day about haulers he had known, done business with, and—for the most part—refused to do business with any more. In his opinion, haulers tend to be either very good or very bad, mostly the latter.

A bad hauler can get an auction operator in trouble fast because it is the operator's reputation with his customers that is on the line. If, for example, the auction operator has advertised that he has a good load coming from

Massachusetts—including several fine old clocks—then bidders will show up expecting a full auction from Massachusetts, to include the fine clocks. Then the hauler shows up with only a part load or perhaps without the promised specific items. Or what if the hauler shows up with a load of nothing but what one operator calls "chicken house" chairs and cheap reproduction glass? Then there are the haulers who will bring a mixed lot—a few good pieces and the rest junk, then proceed to set back the good pieces after using them as come-on bait for the customers. Any of these things makes the operator look bad and understandably hesitant to use the hauler again.

Many haulers who bring in good merchandise are undependable because of personal problems and may, perhaps, show up at the hour of the sale roaring drunk and making a nuisance of themselves. Or they may try to hold the operator up for a guarantee when none was promised at the time the load was contracted for, or they may complain about the prices brought by specific items even if the overall total was good. As one country auction operator told me: "A good hauler asks only 'What have I got in the sale and what is the total that I got?' It is impossible to get exactly what you think you will out of each individual piece."

Still, the hauler remains the country auction's best source of merchandise. This brings up a problem of supply once the traditional sources—New England and the North Central states primarily—have dried up, which is happening faster than the evaporation rate of a small puddle of water in a July Texas sun. Of course, operators of many country auctions get goods elsewhere: at estate sales in neighboring counties or states, bankruptcy sales, and other auctions; but the operator often finds this a more cumbersome way of doing business. It is time consuming, and he must buy this merchandise on his own account, thereby tying up scarce capital until such time that he can resell. Local consignments play a minor role in many country auctions.

The English or European exporters operate in much the same way as pickers except that their hunting grounds are foreign. Too, most foreign exporters rarely consign goods to auction in the United States, but rather sell them to Ameri-

can auction houses; and, instead of hauling their wares about in a truck, they use airplanes and ships. As noted, most "consignments from abroad" are actually foreign goods purchased outright by the auction house and imported into the United States for the sole purpose of auction. In such sales, the house takes the full profit, that is, the difference between what it had to pay for the merchandise (including the cost of transportation) and the selling price.

The import-auction house must provide all the services necessary to get the merchandise from the point of disembarkation to the auction block. This includes clearing the merchandise through customs, transporting it to the house, unpacking, and doing all the chores that accompany any auction.

For most establishments, therefore, providing all the services expected by customers necessitates the maintenance of a building or buildings in which to house merchandise and hold sales and a staff to handle the different stages of the auction. Insurance must be purchased, vehicles serviced, employees trained and compensated, rent and utility bills paid, advertising arranged. The auction itself is but the end result of all this activity, and the people who own and run the auction house are essentially businessmen trying to clear a profit.

I am not suggesting that auction house operators have no feeling for what they are selling. On the contrary, many of them seem to have a genuine affection for what they are doing and the merchandise they handle. Still, good taste and nicety of feeling do not exempt them from business necessities. They must pay their bills as promptly as the mere mover of merchandise; they must solve the same problems as the operator who does view the often beautiful things that go through his establishment as so many widgets to be sold.

A continuing problem in the auction business is the maintenance of a competent staff. It was emphasized to me repeatedly that there are no unimportant jobs in the running of an auction. Each member of the staff must know his or her job and consistently do it well or the entire effort suffers. "You'd be surprised," one operator explained, "how much difference good helpers make in a sale." (Helpers are the people who bring the merchandise to the block and display it.) He was wrong; I wouldn't be surprised at the difference they can make. All auction hounds have been to sales that were handicapped by clumsy, slow, or irritating helpers. Dependable people must be found to pick up consigned articles, and often the helpers handle this chore in a house not large enough to keep a large staff. Bookkeepers must be hired to handle the large amount of financial record keeping involved in the auction. In common with other kinds of businessmen, the auction operator finds it increasingly difficult to get and to keep good people.

Choice and maintenance of premises pose another set of problems. The location of the display and sale hall must be convenient (but convenient to whom, cry some operators?). It must provide adequate parking for patrons; it must be large enough to accommodate enough people for an average-sized sale, yet not so large that maintenance is unduly costly. These days it's a plus if it's convenient to public transportation although most auction houses as yet have reported no real difficulties directly attributable to the im-

pending energy crisis. Building overhead seems to be a particular concern of many auction houses because land rents and utility costs are soaring. Another factor that must be considered in choosing a location is whether or not it will be possible to obtain insurance in this neighborhood without paying extra rating charges.

There is, indeed, as we said earlier, more to running an auction house than immediately meets the eye. In addition to overcoming the difficulties inherent in such complex operations, auction houses must cope with continual rumors attacking the integrity of everyone in the business. These rumors bother auction operators because they are bad for business and also because no one wants to make his living from something held in low general esteem. After you have been to a few auctions, you will probably have heard them all, and no auction house seems to be immune.

After all, everyone *knows:* (1) the auctioneer is in cahoots with the dealers; (2) he pulls bids from thin air in order to run up the final prices; (3) he lies about the authenticity, age, and condition of what he's selling; (4) he buys anything going cheap for the house to resell later for a profit; and (5) he lets the consignors bid. And he does all this at the instigation of the house, which is constantly thinking up new ways to cheat the auctiongoer—or so the story goes.

In the course of researching this book, I've talked with a lot of long-term auctiongoers and several experienced auctioneers. Here are a few of their views on the honesty of auction houses and auctioneers in general:

> This business *has* attracted a class of people who aren't entirely straight.
>
> A lot of the fly-by-night outfits really don't care about the customer. Why should they?
>
> There's a little bit of larceny in all of us, and maybe more than that in the auction business.
>
> Some questionable practices, even fraud, are perhaps inevitable in a business like this one, but I think the consignor suffers from it more frequently than the bidder.

So it may be gathered that the rumors which persist are not entirely groundless, and many people—including some who are irresistibly drawn to auctions—are convinced that Diogenes with a thousand lamps could not find an honest man in this business.

Without attempting to argue this point on the basis of specific instances of fraud or trickery, which definitely occur from time to time (and from which almost all auctiongoers suffer at some point), I'd like to examine these common complaints against the auction house and its employees.

First of all, most states have some laws governing the conduct of public auctions; and if an outfit plans to be around for any length of time, the odds are that it is adhering to at least the minimum standard required by law. In most areas, auction houses are required to state to customers the terms under which they sell. These terms are sometimes posted on the wall or printed in a catalogue, but often they are merely announced at the start of the auction. Few auctiongoers pay much attention to these terms of sale, which is unfortunate since by these terms the house usually announces that it plans to do many of the things that the suspicious public claims are done surreptitiously to defraud the innocent auctiongoer. Understand, I am not defending the trickier practices of auction houses; I am simply saying that there is nothing particularly hidden about them.

Take the business of authenticity, age, and condition. Most houses take pains to inform the audience that every-

thing is sold "as is" and that the auctioneer shall not be held responsible for either genuineness or condition. This means that the auctioneer can sit up there all night and say that this 1927 Montgomery Ward reproduction is an Empire table and risk nothing except his credibility should anyone in the audience know the difference. He can also say that this coffeemaker is "like new" when, in fact, it does not work at all. As far as the auction house is concerned, the auctioneer is talking to hear himself talk; nothing he says binds them or provides any out for the customer should merchandise prove to be something other than what was described.

There are, of course, some auction houses that guarantee that everything is exactly as they represent it. Sotheby's in New York now guarantees that all items are as described, giving the customer five years in which to prove otherwise and demand a refund. Unfortunately, with some lesser houses, a guarantee is worth little, as the purchaser may find that what he thought the auctioneer *meant* in regard to a specific piece was not at all what was *said*. In the long run, the auctiongoer must depend on his own judgment of age and condition. This reluctance to adhere to the strict truth may not be good manners on the part of the house. It would certainly be more thoughtful if the auctioneer would say, "This isn't really very good, but we do wish you'd buy it." Such candor would be a refreshing and welcome change, but is unlikely unless consumerism gains control of the auction business.

As for the auctioneer being in cahoots with the dealers, this may happen at times; but for the most part, they are natural combatants. The auctioneer trying to squeeze the last little advance out of a tight-fisted dealer and the dealer trying to hold to his own predetermined expenditure limit are engaged in a sort of race, with the object on the block as the prize. Yet the prize goes to the loser—the auctioneer getting to award it to someone else or the dealer having to spend perhaps more than he'd planned to get it. Interestingly enough, both consignors and auctiongoers complain about the auctioneer-dealer conspiracies. The consignors often feel that the auctioneer will let things go to pet dealers too cheaply, while the auctiongoers vow that pet dealers run up the price as a favor to the auctioneer.

Do auctioneers pull bids from thin air? Sometimes, and in the case of opening bids probably quite often. One operator justified the fabricated opening bid by saying that most people are reluctant to open merchandise for fear of appearing foolish and that his auctioneer often opens bidding without any help from the audience, which invariably responds by continuing the bidding. Another auctioneer said that he fabricated the opening bid just to keep things moving faster. Do auctioneers see bids that don't exist once the bidding has begun? Unfortunately, some do. There is one well known auction company in the South that does it so openly that it is more of a joke than anything else. This outfit's auctioneer will put up a piece of furniture and run its price up to a predetermined level, hoping naturally that someone will join in with a genuine bid. In the event that this fortuitous circumstance does not occur, the piece is nevertheless knocked down as sold, then—in full view of the audience—put back in the unsold stack.

What may seem like pulling bids from out of nowhere is sometimes the auctioneer's exercising his right—usually announced or published in the terms of sale—to bid on behalf of the consignor. This is a form of hidden reserve and protects the consignor from bargain hunters. Many auctiongoers find this practice particularly infuriating and say that they would prefer that the auctioneer admit that a reserve of so much has been placed on the item and try to get someone to bid above that sum. In a way, it does seem self-defeating for an auctioneer to start an item far below its reserve price. Still, a good auctioneer can often, once an item has been started, coax enough genuine bids from an audience to reach the reserve price when an announced reserve might kill all initial enthusiasm on the part of the bidders. As seller, the consignor has the right to place a value on his goods and to demand that the house not sell them for less than a certain minimum; and once the reserve is set by the consignor, the house may not sell below that price.

I attended an auction recently where the person next to me fumed through half the sale because she was convinced that the auctioneer had bid against her on a large art glass vase. In the catalogue which whe waved about so angrily, neatly printed under "Conditions of Sale Applicable to Buyers," it was plainly set forth that the auctioneer "may bid on the vendor's behalf for all goods which are being offered subject to a reserve or at the Auctioneer's discretion."

Reserves, stated or otherwise, are a sore spot with many auctiongoers, yet they make good sense from the point of view of both the consignor and the house. It is very well for an auctioneer to announce—as did one I heard last fall—"We want you to get bargains." It sounds good, but it would read more truthfully that the house wants you to get enough bargains so that you'll keep coming back; the rest of your buys make the sale possible. If everything sold for bargain prices, then the auction house would not be in business for long, as consignors would be reluctant to bring goods to the block.

Whenever I hear someone griping about the unfairness of reserves, I am reminded of the episode in 1773 in London when Thomas Chippendale and several other well known cabinetmakers managed to confuse other creditors of a customer for whom they had all worked and not been paid. As a result of the successful duplicity concerning the bankruptcy auction of the customer's belongings, only a few bidders attended the sale; and Chippendale and his co-conspirators managed to buy the extravagant lady's valuable property for a fraction of its worth, thereby defrauding all of the other creditors and coming out much to the good themselves. This is not to say that modern auctiongoers are out to defraud anyone, although one auction operator claims that 85 percent of the auction must "appeal to man's desire to get something for nothing" in order to succeed.

Another point of contention is whether or not consignors should be allowed to bid on their own property. Actually there is little that the auctioneer can do to prevent the consignor from protecting his interest in this way. There was a landmark legal decision on this particular point in 1934 when an appellate court in New York ruled that the American Art Association–Anderson Galleries had denied a consignor his rights in not letting him bid when his own property was on the block, basing its decision on the fact that the words "unrestricted public sale" had appeared in advertis-

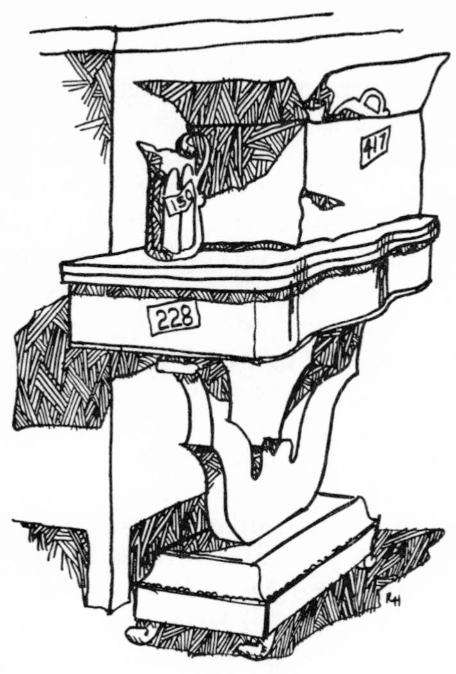

ing. Since most auctions announce that they are "unrestricted" or that "merchandise will be sold to the highest bidder" without defining what is meant by the term "bidder," the consignor has a perfect right to bid.

The question of house buying or selling on its own account raises a more complex issue of ethics. Many auction houses operate retail and sometimes wholesale outlets as a sideline, so it is not unnatural that some of their merchandise should turn up at auction. Most auction houses try to avoid this, as they can rarely get a price at auction equal to the price they can get by selling the merchandise over the counter. Sometimes, however, when the auction is going to run short, the shop may be raided for likely auctionables. Also, the auction makes a handy dumping ground when the shop wants to clean out old stock. As for buying at its own auction, either to take advantage of bargains or to up the overall price level, this is perhaps a bit stickier. The house that does this with any degree of regularity will wind up short on customers, commissions, and consignors and long on miscellaneous stock. Still, some houses do buy for their own account, usually to resell at a subsequent auction.

Houses that do not sell their own goods at auction say that the practice is bad business, that the temptation is always there to inflate values artificially, and in much stronger degree than exists when a commission is all that is at stake.

Oddly enough, a quite common form of intentional misrepresentation goes unnoticed by even the most gimlet-eyed auctiongoers much of the time. For its success, this bit of trickery depends on the American fascination with great or at least notorious names. A rose is not necessarily a rose, in spite of Gertrude Stein. The garden in which it grew had a decided effect on its market price. And the garden of a well known collector or a celebrity can produce a rose that will sell for a lot more than can the garden of Joe Blah.

This is why nimble-footed, transient auction operators go about the country, advertising that they will auction articles from the estate of the well-known collector Mrs. Whitney Vanderbilt Rockerfeller Stickpin, long recognized for her perceptiveness in nosing out the finest of Americana or Sandwich glass or whatever. In small type at the bottom of such ads may often be seen the words "plus additions," a nicety required by law in some areas since in reality only two or three out of one hundred items in the sale were actually "perceived" by Mrs. Stickpin. And do you think that the people at that auction are going to be disabused of the notion that whatever is on the block was one of her dearest treasures? Not on your auction number, they're not. In fact, the auctioneer will do everything possible to intimate that it was—without actually saying so, of course.

It was once common practice in Pennsylvania, where the auction business has always been extremely competitive and even cutthroat, for crafty operators to go to a well known family (preferably with an historic name) in distressed financial condition but still hanging onto the ancestral home and to offer them a thousand dollars or so for the use of their house for a sale. The operator would then advertise that an auction of fine old antiques and miscellany would take place in the old So-and-So mansion on a certain date. Everyone would assume that the merchandise was really from the house, and many people would come to see the house and to buy something primarily because of the family involved. All the auction house did, of course, was to stack whatever was left of the genuine family possessions in the attic or a back part of the house, then fill the rest of the house with merchandise brought in from its own premises.

If all of these little misrepresentations and big evasions and endless reservations are going to infuriate you, perhaps you are not temperamentally equipped to play the auction game. Because, like it or not, it's the auction house's ballground, and to a large extent the auction house makes the rules. Your only protection lies in how well you understand the rules and your own motives for auctiongoing.

When it comes down to it, say some auction house proprietors, many auctiongoers don't play a very honest game themselves. They spread falsehoods about certain merchandise or lots on which they hope to bid themselves, thereby anticipating and often getting the lots for a lower price. They try to refuse responsibility for items on which they successfully bid. They sign a false name and address on the register book. They pass bad checks. They even steal. Admittedly, the number of auctiongoers who do these things is in the minority, but then so are the crooked auction houses—as most professional auctioneers and operators claim.

"Most of the people who've been in this any length of time are straight with their customers. If you're not reasonably ethical, you won't last long. People aren't stupid, you know," pointed out one auction proprietor. "At least my customers aren't. Most of them probably know as much about this business as I do."

"I always think of what Sam Meadows—he was, to my way of thinking, the forerunner of a lot of the country auctions you see around today—told me when I was starting in the business," remembered one successful operator. "He said, 'If you run it straight, there'll be about 50 percent of the people who'll believe you, and that'll be enough. If you run it crooked, 50 percent will think you're crooked anyway, and the other 50 percent will find you out sooner or later.' "

But what can the auction professionals, as they like to think of themselves, do to convince the public of their self-proclaimed integrity? How can they combat rumors of house-inflated bids, for instance?

"That's why I like noisy bidders," declared one country auctioneer. "That way there's no question about who is bidding and who gets what."

One way of combating the rumors of crookedness is to act promptly when the opportunity arises. When a prominent New England auctioneer was asked what he did when a bidder asked him the name of a competing bidder, the implication being that there was no competing bidder, this long-time professional replied, "I immediately knock the item down to the other bidder or to whoever made the last bid if there are more than two people bidding, even if the bid isn't as high as I might like. The other bidder has the right to privacy, and no loud mouth is going to put me on the spot like that."

Another auction operator says that, "If people trusted auction houses, you couldn't get in the door." But no one seems to know exactly what to do to stop the rumors or to remedy the conditions that give rise to them except to be as straight as possible and to make sure that the audience understands anything that might look questionable. Most professionals seem to feel that this is a matter of common sense as much as of business ethics. Or, more succinctly put, it means survival as a going establishment.

It is the attempt to juggle three diverse, not always compatible, sets of interests that forces the auction house into postures not always pleasing to either consignor or auction-goer and that tempts the unscrupulous proprietor or auctioneer into dishonest practices. For this there seems no remedy.

It may be true that many auction operators share the sentiments expressed by one voluble auctioneer: "We want you to get good buys and leave happy. That's the idea of public auction." Yet the satisfied bidder is only one of three important objectives, the other two being a consignor who feels that he has been treated fairly and the continued solvency of the auction house. The individual operator's ability to balance these sometimes conflicting interests determines the ultimate success of his establishment. As one operator put it, "Sleight of hand ought to be required training for anybody crazy enough to go into the auction business."

Chapter 4

The Auctioneer

The antiques auction sells glamor, or at least color, as much as it sells merchandise. It is a show as well as a sale. The undoubted star of this show is the auctioneer, a fact recognized by the individual followings of many auctioneers. From the cool elegance of the legendary Hiram Parke to the folksiness of the country auctioneer, it is the auctioneer's distinctive style, personality, and appearance that characterize and, as far as the audience is concerned, help to make the sale what it is.

To extend the theatre analogy, no matter how efficiently and effectively the show is staged, an auctioneer not up to his role is like the inept actor who can negate months of backstage effort by flubbing his cues on opening night. This is a big responsibility; the auctioneer, unlike the actor, must depend on his own wits for what he says and does. He must control the sale so that at its conclusion everyone—the consignors, the house, and the audience—is as well satisfied as can be reasonably expected. Prerequisites of this control are his knowledge of values and his ability to interpret a particular audience's mood.

Such knowledge and ability are not gifts from the auctioneer's god, but must be acquired in one way or another and used to support the instinct for drama and sense of timing that all successful auctioneers seem to possess. How does a person prepare for auctioneering?

There are schools of auctioneering which—judging from their promotional material—draw their students mostly from the ranks of people dissatisfied with their present occupations and looking for an easier, more profitable job. At these schools, the would-be auctioneer is instructed in sales management and advertising, laws pertaining to auctions, speech, psychology, and judgment of values. Resident courses last from eight days to two weeks and may be supplemented by home study. As of now, their cost is around $250, which includes some living expenses while attending the school. Upon graduation from these schools, the fledgling auctioneers are styled Colonel and—again according to

the advertising material put out by some of the schools—immediately don the Colonel's wide-brimmed hat and embark upon a sea of auctions, which their training at the school enables them to handle successfully.

Although these necessarily concentrated courses doubtless offer a lot of valuable insight into the conduct of an auction, they seem designed to attract would-be cattle or automobile auctioneers rather than those who aspire to wield the gavel over antiques sales. You will see a few of these graduates conducting country auctions, but most antiques auctioneers learn their craft through a more painstaking process, the timeworn method of apprenticeship.

When a newcomer to the business boasted to the well known Ira Reed some years ago, "Well, I'm an auctioneer now," Ira replied, "No, but after ten years you may *become* an auctioneer." A quick look at the backgrounds of America's better known auctioneers tends to bear out this opinion. Louis Marion, for instance, began at the old American Art Association in New York as a mail clerk. He worked his way up to become a record clerk, then ultimately succeeded Hiram Parke behind the rostrum at Parke-Bernet.

The job of record clerk, very important in itself to the success of the auction, is regarded as a natural lead-in to auctioneering. Since the clerk sits beside or near the auctioneer, facing the audience, keeping records on each item sold, and often helping to spot bids, he is in an excellent position to observe not only the auctioneer's techniques at close hand, but also the reaction of the crowd and its bidding patterns—all of which will serve him well when he himself is at the microphone trying to convince a reluctant bidder to go one step further.

If this sounds like a slow, even tedious process, it is; but in the course of it, a man acquires the confidence born of a minute knowledge of his field. He becomes less a mere caller of bids and more the translator of the alluring, but often alien language whispered by the object on the block. He has learned enough about himself and his own ability to have evolved an approach to auctioneering that—with appropriate variations for the lot and the crowd—will work for him and will stamp his sales as his and his alone. He can tell when someone is really bidding or just scratching her head and when that person so firmly nodding "no" really means, "I probably will, but give me a minute." He knows when to urge, when to desist. In other words, he knows more about this auction and its potential than anyone else in the room. He is the expert, and it shows and is rewarded by the attentiveness and ungrudging or even wary respect of the crowd.

Apart from acknowledging that a "good" auctioneer is a successful one in that he moves merchandise at a price generally satisfactory to all concerned and at a pace that permits conclusion of the sale before cock's crow, it is impossible to describe this unusual creature with any degree of precision. He may dress in the latest style from London or Rome or conduct a sale in shirt sleeves with arm bands while wearing a black derby hat pushed onto the back of his head. His voice may be well modulated, almost soft, and only gently persuasive; or his shout may be raspy, designed to force the sale onward by its grating quality. His manner may be anything from affected friendliness to aggressive hostility toward both the audience and what he is selling. He may concentrate almost entirely on the object on the block in his patter, or he may banter with the crowd. He may be dignified, even faintly righteous, or he may suggest the barnyard and its natural functions. He may be anything at all—as long as he knows what he is doing; and when he does, he is a delight to watch.

Most regular auctiongoers have preferences in auctioneering styles. Mine is for the quieter approach exercised by someone who either knows what he is selling or has enough sense to keep his mouth shut if he doesn't. At the other extreme, you have what I think of as tobacco auctioneers, whom some addicts consider indispensable to a real country auction. I have a friend who enjoys the auctioneer with a sarcastic approach to both merchandise and audience. Some people, quite often those who view the auction almost entirely as a show rather than a sale, dote on the auctioneer with the endless repertoire of jokes, usually faintly blue and having little to do with auctions, the merchandise on the block, or the people there to buy it. The folksy, fatherly auctioneer has a definite following; many people like his quaint speech and determinedly humble ways.

The Auctioneer

After you have been to a few different auctions, you will have encountered most of the basic types of auctioneers; and as you continue to go, you will have an opportunity to see many variations of each style and to develop inevitable preferences of your own.

As might be expected, you will generally find the more urbane auctioneers handling the showier estate and import sales, the folksier ones selling garden variety estates and average imports; and if you see our friend in the derby with a cigar clamped between his teeth, you can expect a lot of fruit jars and rusted farm implements. Each of these auctioneers will have his own way of working up bids.

There is, for example, the offhand, even deprecatory approach: "My goodness, this is an odd-looking lot of stuff, but since you folks are a lot smarter than I am, you know what to do with it. It's probably not worth it, but will you give me $5? See, I told you you'd know what to do with it; who'll give me $10?"

There is the personal plea: "Now folks, if I don't get more than that for this fine piece, they're gonna show me the door. Things tonight have been that bad. I got $10; who'll make it $15?"

There is the demand: "This is top quality merchandise, worth at least twice what's been bid. $50 is all I have; someone make it $75."

There is the confidential approach: "Just between us, this desk was appraised at twice that price. Frankly, I think it's a mistake to let it go for this, but my instruction was to sell everything tonight regardless of price. I surely hate to see this go for just $200, but someone is getting a real bargain. Anybody go $225?"

There is the insult: "I thought you people were here for an auction. If you're not, go on home. If you are, somebody give me $25 for this clock."

There is version one of the implied compliment: "I don't have to tell *you* what this epergne is worth, so who will go to $2,000?"

And version two: "I thought *you* people wanted quality, and I only have $100 for this beautiful oil. Will you bid $125?"

Of course, they're all saying the same thing: "Give me more money for this item on the block." If they have analyzed their crowd correctly, whatever approach the auctioneers choose will work. There are potential bidders who will be intimidated enough by the insult, flattered enough by the implied compliment, or impressed enough by the confidential appraisal to go beyond their tentative limit. You will notice that auctioneers will vary their plea from sale to sale, subtly altering it for each particular group of people. Still, the basic approach—be it friendliness or impatience—will generally remain the same.

The same distinctiveness characterizes the way that different auctioneers call bids. Some of them rattle the call so fast that no one but an experienced hand can follow the sale; others just sort of drawl along until the proceedings drag to a halt and the item is sold. There is a whole school of auctioneering that gargles bids. Since calling bids can vary so much and is the source of confusion for many auctiongoers, I thought it would be interesting to record—word for word—the actual calls of several different auctioneers. Here are nine of these calls, with thumbnail sketches of their originators.

At a classy auction sponsored by a cultural group, the auctioneer was so well dressed, well tanned, and well spoken that he made the most elegant member of his bejeweled, champagne-sipping audience seem gauche. His manner was as smooth as he was (well almost):

> Here's a nice silver and crystal cruet, possibly late Georgian I'd say. Who will open this cruet at $100? I have $50. I am bid $50. Will you make it $60? $60. $70. $80. $90. $90, I am bid $90. Will you make it $100? $100? $100. $110. $120. $130. $140. You use a lot of oil and vinegar here, right? $150? Who will make it $150? $150. Good for you, sir. $160? $160. $170. $180. $190. I am bid $190; will you make it $200? $200? I am bid $200; will you make it $210? No? Anyone else $210? $210? Sold to the gentleman on the aisle for $200.

An auction of modern oils, lithographs, etchings, and

watercolors produced a plump, young auctioneer in an ill-fitting, rumpled suit, his voice sounding like syrup poured from a warm jar.

> This is an original color etching. Signed, numbered, out of print now. A gold leaf frame. A beautiful etching. If you'd like to have it, open up quickly at $25. Quickly bid $30. $35. Quickly bid $40. $45. Quickly bid $50. At $50; give me $52.50. At $50; bid $52.50. At $52.50, bid $55. Round it off at $60. Quickly bid $62.50. At $62.50, bid $65. $65 in time. You bid $67.50 in time. $70 quickly, quickly. Sold for $67.50 to No. 3.

At a clearance sale for an auction house specializing in imports of varying quality, the auctioneer was a short dark man, well but casually dressed. His voice was slightly twangy, and he wisecracked almost constantly:

> O.K. Here's a slot machine, working. Just like Vegas; a one-armed bandit. For the game machine, the one-armed bandit, who'll give me a $100 start. $50? Who'll go $50? $35? Who'll go $25? $25! Will you go $50? I got $30 in two places at least. I'm bid $30 only, now $35. Will you go $35? $35 I have, $35 only. Will you go $40? $40? $40? Will you go $40? $40 I got. Will you go $50? Great for playroom or den. Invite your friends over to play, help pay for the house. $50, I got $50. Will you go $60? I have $55, will you go $60? $60, will you go $60? Last call for $60. Sold for $55 to No. 16.

A man in a poorly tailored business suit, who would have looked more at home behind the desk of a finance company than on his auctioneer's stool, was handling a large sale of relatively high quality import merchandise. His voice was low, almost inaudible at times. His bid calling reads much more rhythmically than it sounded at the time:

> Let's put up all the trinket sets together, boys. There are seven of these all told. You're bidding for choice; take one or any number. Now, by the piece, how much for the trinket sets? $10. $12.50. $15. $17.50. $20. $22.50. $22.50, I have. Now $25. $27.50? $27.50?

> Sold for $25 to No. 12. How many you want? Just one? Pick it out, and we'll sell the others by the piece, but high bidder to take the lot. How much by the piece for the lot? $5. $7.50. $10. $12.50. $15. $17.50? $17.50? Then sold for $15 times six. The number is 23.

Presiding over one of the poorest assortments of country auction merchandise ever assembled was a confident young man in shirtsleeves, whose hair was combed back from his face in ducktails, and from whose lips spewed the relentlessly harsh cry of the tobacco-style auctioneer, slowed down for the junque sale audience, but still running at about twice the pace of any other style of auctioneering:

> Here are two brass sconces with amber glass shades. Look to be new. I got $2 now. Half, would you go a half? $2.50 now. Half, would you go a half? $3. Half, half, would you go a half? Half, half, would you go a half? Repeating, three and a half anywhere? Last call. $3 it is. No. 4.

Another young auctioneer, just as confident, but considerably more suave in his presentation, was dressed in the latest Italian knit as he handled a relatively small sale of high quality imports. His voice was low, but always audible, his manner unhurried:

> The first lot up tonight is an opaque porcelain plate, circa 1830. How much to start this one? Will you say $5 to start this plate? $5 I have. And $6? I've got $5; will you say $6? $6 and $7. And $8? Will you say $8? Beautiful condition. $8 I have. And $9? $9 I have. And $10? $10. $11? $11? I've got $10 on the right. $11? $11? $10 to No. 21.

An attractive, casually dressed man auctioned a large lot of primitives at a big city gallery, making no attempt to "hoke up" the proceedings, simply scaling his presentation to the completely different sort of audience that is attracted to such sales. In a fairly slow-paced, easily understandable voice, he disposed of the merchandise in a manner totally lacking in either pretension or condescension:

> Next is No. 256. The child's high chair. Here's a cutie, an old one too. Nice leg and back. Who'll say $25 to start? $10 I have. Who'll say $12.50? $15? $16? $17? $18? $19? $20? We should have started here. A rarity. Are we all through here. A rare chair. $21? $22? $23? $24? Are you sure? $25? $26? $26 now? I have $25. $26? $27? $27? $26, No. 343.

Conducting an estate sale of lots of widely varying quality was an obviously experienced, fastidiously groomed older man who expertly but calmly moved the sale along with his dulcet tones:

> Lot No. 352 coming up. Here we have a seven piece set. It consists of two settees and five chairs: two arm, three side. Cabriole legs. It's a set I would assume could be about 1875-1890. Somewhere about there. Seven pieces in all. How much to start it? Nobody wants it? Who'll say $300? $200? Well, let's start it somewhere. Who'll say $100? Good, who'll say $150? Then $125. Should be that a piece. $150. I call this a bargain. $175? Who'll say $175? All through at $150? I thought it'd bring a lot more than that. $175 over there? All through at $150? It is sold then at $150. The number is 39.

I will not waste your time reproducing the sale of one of the draggy lots featured by many auction houses where time and tide are forced to wait for every man, where there are no guideposts for the buyer, and where the final price usually reflects the degree of irritation that the auctioneer or floor man is able to engender to force up the bid. Out of curiosity, I timed one such lot at an auction house where the floor man is the boss and can show the merchandise as long as he wants before indicating to his auctioneer to move on. It took this particular item, which was a small tattered jewel box full of costume jewelry, three minutes to sell for $12.50. The tobacco-style auctioneer can move as many as two items a minute—at least the several that I timed did on occasion; and even the most relaxed auctioneer will usually sell an item every two minutes or so unless the crowd is sluggish.

Several old auction hands kind enough to share their auction experiences vow that the auctioneer at most houses always tries to start the item for two or three times what it is worth, hoping at best that someone who doesn't know its value will jump in and at worst that the opening bid will be high in relation to the object's value. Like so many old "truths," this is not borne out by actual circumstances.

Over a period of months, I monitored sales conducted by several different auctioneers, trying to compile statistics on at least three sales by each man, to see if there is indeed a correlation between the auctioneer's suggested opening bid, the actual opening bid, the final bid, and the object's value. The only conclusion that I reached is that sometimes there is a correlation and sometimes there is not, depending on the auctioneer.

If the auctioneer is inexperienced and does not know values, then there will certainly be no correlation between any of these figures. Since he does not know the object's value, his suggested opening bid is off, and the opening bid that he ultimately accepts bears no relation to either the object's value or the auctioneer's suggested opening bid. I have noticed a tendency in such auctioneers to try to start all small items—vases, platters, decanters, and the like—at $10 to $20, while most articles or furniture draw $25 to $50 most frequently. If no one jumps in to bid $20 on the platter (which may be worth $2 or $30) or $50 on the table (which may be worth $10 or $100), such auctioneers usually take almost anything as an opening bid. As long as people bid readily, bidding continues. When bidding stops, this auctioneer will usually move along, making little or no attempt to elicit further bids even if the last bid was obviously far below the object's value. The only protection such an auctioneer has lies with the proprietor, who can either provide him with a list of minimum acceptable prices ahead of time on key items or can signal when something is going too low.

If the auctioneer knows values, but consistently treats the suggested opening bid as a joke, there is no correlation between this figure and the actual opening and final bids. There may, however, be a correlation between what he accepts as the actual opening bid, the object's value, and the final selling price. On a vase worth, say $50 retail, one auctioneer might say: "Who'll give me $300 for this gorgeous vase? Ha, ha. It's a beaut. No takers at $300? Then who'll give me $25? $15? $10? $10, I have. . . ." Then the vase might be worked up to a price close to the true value. With such an auctioneer, the suggested opening bid reflects nothing but his own sense of the ridiculous and perhaps that shot of Scotch which he grabbed before the sale began.

Some auctioneers, who may or may not know values, never suggest opening bids except on lots with stated reserve prices or on lots that no one would start at any price unless urged. In effect, such an auctioneer lets an object find its own level with a particular group of bidders. Actual opening bids are usually extremely low in relation to the object's value at the sales of auctioneers utilizing this approach; but final prices—oddly enough—tend to be consistently higher at such sales.

There are, however, auctioneers who adhere to a pattern in their suggested opening bids. One auctioneer, for example, inevitably starts a lot by asking for about twice what the object is worth, then takes an actual opening bid of approximately one-half of the object's value, selling finally for a price close to value. Another auctioneer whom I monitored regularly tries to start the object for one-half of its value; and if that doesn't work, he drops to one-quarter value, then works the price up to a reasonable level. Still another auctioneer suggests a price, then drops to one-half or even one-quarter of that price to open; but the majority of the time the final bid is within 15 percent of the suggested opening bid. When asked about this, he admitted that the initial price suggestion is his candid, on-the-spot appraisal of the object's value.

All of this suggested opening bid rigamarole may seem pointless to you; but if you do not know values, spotting a particular auctioneer's bid calling pattern can afford you a small measure of guidance and protection against being taken. When you're attending an unfamiliar auction, you can quickly get an idea of the pattern by watching the sale of eight to ten lots and comparing the suggested opening bid, actual opening bid, and final bid. If you do know values, spotting this pattern will give you an idea of the house's estimate of an object's worth and also whether or not the auctioneer is knowledgeable about the merchandise that he is selling.

The most visible part of an auctioneer's style is his patter, the odd talk with which he instructs or amuses or, sometimes, irritates the audience. Many auctiongoers are great connoisseurs of patter and, indeed, judge an auctioneer by his skill in this department.

There are auctioneers who know the merchandise that

they are selling so well that their comments provide a capsulized education in fine and applied art. It was at an auction of modern art that I heard a clearer and certainly more concise explanation of the difference between lithographs and etchings, mezzotints and engravings than I ever got in school or read in reference books.

Other auctioneers, usually those specializing in the tonier sales, like to instruct the audience in a slightly different fashion, emphasizing the past ownership of a particular object and the fact that people of cultural refinement have always considered this period the most superlative in design. People of fashion, for instance, love the work of eighteenth-century French *ébénistes* and Aubusson rugs; the furniture of these masters and the honeyed colors of these rugs—says this auctioneer—are found in the most elegant homes. In this sort of pitch, you will hear a lot of "They say" and "You should" and very little about the article in question.

Still another sort of auctioneer will pay very little attention to either the article on the block or to its possible past except to use it as the butt of a joke or the takeoff point for some personal philosophizing. This auctioneer will usually spend a lot of time establishing a "down home" atmosphere, interrupting the bidding to ask if Mr. Brown got his car fixed all right the other day or to tell a joke on one of the auctiongoers. Like all patter, this kind can backfire so that it becomes less an amusing sidelight and more an impediment to the progress of the sale. As one auction operator remarked of an attractive school-trained auctioneer: "He had a lot of country philosophy about him. But he spent too much time on country philosophy and too little on selling. The crowd got restless."

In a negative sense, there is a kind of auctioneer who is denied "patter privilege." He may open the sale by making a few random remarks, but after that he will confine himself to calling bids and occasionally commenting briefly when a price seems very low. If you watch, the reason becomes quickly apparent. The floor man, that is, the man who directs and sometimes displays the merchandise, is the boss. It is he who will loudly preach the virtues of the lots that he

waves about in front of the audience and sometimes in front of its individual and collective noses. It is he who will get disgusted with a slow bidding pattern and yell, "Sell it, sell it, we gotta move on." As may be guessed, it is his auction house, and his auctioneer has little authority to do anything but call bids. Any patter must come from the floor man, as must any response to the audience. This division of responsibility and management sometimes works, but more often doesn't, as the audience seems to sense the ambiguity of the situation. This auctioneer is like the captain of a ship whose owner shares its deck.

In most cases, though, it is the auctioneer who must make the sale and the auctioneer who must bear the responsibility. It is up to him to say whatever will make this object seem most appealing to this group of people and to make them willing to compete for its possession, and he must decide when he has milked the last available bid on it.

Along with most auctiongoers, I am curious about the man up there with the microphone and the bemused expression. What is he like? We know what we think about him; what does he think about us? And what are his real feelings about the things that he sells? Does he ever get hooked on them, or is he so sick of *things* that he sits on orange crates and eats off paper plates? As has been suggested, many different kinds of people take up auctioneering. In the first place, although I have used the masculine pronoun throughout this book for the sake of convenience, the auctioneer may be male or female. At the moment, men greatly outnumber women in this profession, but the women are slowly gaining. The auctioneer may be any age from puberty onwards. His general education may have ended with grammar school, or he may hold university degrees. His qualifications for auctioneering may derive from experience, formal training, or a combination of both.

He may be the model of integrity or one step away from incarceration. His honesty is questioned with monotonous regularity, and he must react to such challenges without hampering his conduct of the sale. For obvious reasons, he tends to be a poised, confident individual whose personality projects well before an audience. He usually has a very

audible—if not always pleasant—voice. He must be persuasive and have the presence of manner to reinforce his authority over the audience and the merchandise.

He is often physically attractive, whatever his age. He may be a stable family man, or he may be a drifter who cannot go on until he is almost drunk. He has the stamina to endure the concentrated, tension-producing demands made by all but the most unimportant sales. Above all else, if he is to be successful, he must have the intelligence to sense the mood and potential of every auction and the adaptability to gear his own efforts to capitalize on each sale's unique opportunities.

He may be the principal of the house for which he sells, one of several partners, or a paid employee. If he does share in ownership, he may be compensated according to the house's net profits. If he is a salaried, full-time employee, then his compensation for auctioneering may be included in his regular paycheck. If he is a free-lance auctioneer, he is usually paid either a flat sum for conducting the sale or a small percentage of the sale's gross.

If he is only an employee, not an owner, of the house, he may or may not conduct all of its auctions. Some houses keep a stable of several auctioneers and call on whichever auctioneer has a style appropriate for a given sale. For this reason, many auctioneers try to stretch themselves to acquire a general reputation for handling almost any kind of sale well, while others aim at building a reputation for expertise in a narrower field.

In return for licensing by the state in which he sells and for membership in his professional association, he must agree to abide by the laws of his area and the ethics of his calling; and as a rule he seems to. His chosen occupation is not always easy; but if he is good and is willing to hustle to solicit selling assignments, he can make a good living. If he prefers, he can work another job, handling sales only in his spare time. He need not fear growing old (good auctioneers seem to age like good wine); depressions often improve his business opportunities; and as yet he has no need to worry about automation.

If the auctioneers that I observed and interviewed are

typical, the auctioneer respects the knowledgeable, courteous auctiongoer, but seems bound by no scruples in his treatment of the ignorant and rude. Sometimes his empathy for what he is selling is quite clear, as is his frequent contempt. Sometimes it is equally clear that the object on the block interests him not at all.

Some auctioneers collect (although—they claim—not through their own sales); others do not. Some of them live in high-rise apartments furnished in the spirit of Mies, others in Edwardian mansions in which Edith Wharton would feel at home.

The auctioneer may be, feel, think, or have almost anything. He is, in fact, quite like the audiences that he faces—save that he is the hunter and we are the prey.

Chapter 5

Preparations for Sale

Every auction has its own particular character. There are friendly auctions, and there are businesslike auctions. There are casual auctions and auctions where formality is the keynote. There are fun auctions and auctions in deadly earnestness. There are collector's auctions and junk auctions.

From the time you see or hear the first advertisement until you walk away from the sale with your acquisition, an auction will have impressed its particular character upon you. The way in which it is advertised hints at its nature, as does its sponsorship. The kind of place in which it is being held adds to this effect. The assortment and condition of goods and the manner in which they are displayed confirm your initial impression.

Each auction must, so to speak, create its own environment. It does this partly by the manner in which the auction itself is handled and partly by the sort of preparations that the house has chosen or been allowed to make for the sale. Creation of the proper environment has as its desired result the highest possible price for the items that will go on the block. To effect this creation, the auction house must make a number of decisions regarding every sale.

How many decisions depends on the auction and the kind of auction house involved. If a civic group, for example, hires an auction house to handle only the sale itself, assembly of the merchandise and details of preparation are the concern of the sponsor, not the house. The group itself must decide the audience it will be able to attract and what kind of merchandise will prompt the auctiongoers to part with the most money. It must also decide how to advertise to reach this prospective group. The auction house may provide the auctioneer, the record clerk, the cashier, and floor men. These personnel will sell the merchandise and collect the monies. Often, the house is not only presented with the assembled auction, but also with the terms under which it may sell. Here, the auction agent has few decisions to make in advance of the sale itself.

Some kinds of auction establishments have limited options. The country auction that depends almost entirely on haulers, for example, usually has little choice in the assembly of any particular auction, beyond asking a hauler to bring a load of merchandise of a certain age and condition. The country auction house must sell whatever is brought by the hauler, as it is brought, since few establishments of this sort have enough storage to hold items for later sale. Also, the practice followed by most haulers of arriving barely ahead of the audience precludes any form of a published list or any attempt at any but the most primitive display of merchandise.

For the most part, however, the average auction house faces a series of decisions concerning every sale. What shall be sold and in what sequence? How much work should go into preparing the merchandise for sale? Should a catalogue or list of the merchandise be published for distribution to the public? How should the merchandise be displayed for the pre-sale exhibition? How and to whom should the auction be advertised? When should the sale be held? Should refreshments be served? Which auctioneer should be employed to handle the sale?

First, how should an auction be assembled? Should the

auction house sell all merchandise in the order in which it comes in, so that each auction is the creation of happenstance? Or should the house attempt a more coherent approach, putting merchandise with other items of like kind or quality and reserving the best consignments for special sales? In other words, should consistency within the sale be the aim of the auction assembly?

Many auction houses follow this practice, which has the advantage of concentrating the best merchandise in periodic auctions sure to attract serious collectors able and willing to pay good prices for high quality merchandise. The specialized auction has the added advantage of simplifying advertising, enabling the house to direct promotion of the sale to the people who have already shown an interest in a certain kind or quality of merchandise. Grouping merchandise into compatible assortments, whether these be of quality or kind, has a secondary benefit. A customer interested primarily in nineteenth-century English porcelain will not find himself bored in the midst of a sale of twentieth-century American furniture. Someone wanting a

casual wall hanging for a playroom will not wind up being intimidated by a sale of sixteenth-century Italian art.

Some of the well known auction houses handling big volumes of merchandise auction in groups as a matter of policy. Sometimes these groups even follow a day pattern: books and painting, for instance, on the second Tuesday of every month; nineteenth-century furniture on the first Monday; Art Nouveau on the third Friday.

Specialized sales admittedly have certain disadvantages from the viewpoint of the house. The establishment that has reserved its best consignments or acquisitions for months for a really spectacular auction is risking a lot on one throw of the dice. On the night of the big sale, the weather may be severe enough to discourage many would-be auctiongoers but not rough enough to justify a cancellation of the sale. The economic or political news may be bad that day, so people may not be in a buying mood. Or maybe the sale just doesn't quite jell, so that prices are generally low.

The house which groups merchandise by kind limits the potential appeal of its individual sales by restricting them—in effect—to auctiongoers who already know they like a certain kind of article. In a way, as mentioned earlier, this is good; but it precludes impulse buying by people who came to the sale thinking they were after something quite different from what they wound up buying.

The next decision facing the auction house is the extent to which merchandise will be prepared for sale. Will it be cleaned? Will the house make minor repairs, such as the replacement of broken mirrors? Will the better pieces be treated to restoration and refinishing? Or will the merchandise be sold "as is" or "in the rough," implying major or minor defects?

Part of the house's decision in this regard is based on who will pay for the work done to merchandise. If the merchandise is consigned, the consignor must be willing to pay the cost of any repairs. If the house owns the merchandise, then the cost must come from its own operating budget.

Some auction houses do not receive merchandise in time to do anything to it. Others have a policy of doing nothing, no matter how long they hold the merchandise before sale. Far from protesting, many auctiongoers seem not to mind merchandise "as is" or even "rough."

It cannot be denied that there are people who actually prefer this sort of merchandise, much as there are travelers who find ruins infinitely more interesting than a mansion standing intact. These auctiongoers like visualizing what a piece can become and prefer conjecture about what a little imaginative and loving care can do.

Some auctiongoers are suspicious of a sale where the merchandise is too glossy, seeming to feel that prices will be disproportionately higher to make allowance for the work that the house has put into the preparation. These cynical souls feel that the house is more likely to run up the bid on such merchandise. At a recent auction in Tennessee, I overheard one latecomer whisper loudly to his compan-

ion, "Oh-oh, we might as well go. They've shined all the brass."

Auction houses that do not prepare merchandise can point to attitudes such as these for justification. If some of the people don't really want "gussied-up" goods, why go to a lot of trouble to provide them? Expensive preparation is always a gamble. As one well known auction house principal told me: "I don't think it pays, from the standpoint of the auction house, to put merchandise in the best condition. The house doesn't lose money, but it doesn't gain anything. Too, reconditioning of merchandise isn't always to the benefit of the auctiongoer. After all, once the house has refinished a piece, the purchaser does not know to what extent it has been altered."

Merchandise in obviously dirty or rough condition need not necessarily pose a problem to a clever auctioneer, who can turn what superficially appears a drawback into an advantage. I remember one sale when a beautifully contrived mahogony combination bed steps and chamber pot container was put up. It was so dirty that dust flew visibly when the helpers picked it up and the marks of their hands showed plainly when they set it down on the block. One of the men ostentatiously produced a white handkerchief and proceeded to blacken it with dirt from his hand. Laughing as loudly as anyone in the audience, the auctioneer turned to the steps and commented, "You can see the beauty of the satinwood cross-banding even through *that* dust. Imagine what it'd be shined up." The audience ate it up; and by using humor directed at the house, the auctioneer was able to establish good rapport with the audience early in the sale, as well as to move the piece of furniture at a better price.

At another sale, the auctioneer watched his floor man drop an ornate majolica jar which promptly shattered into six large sections, then drawled, "What am I bid for this kit? It'll give you something to do tomorrow."

While some houses are quite unconcerned about the condition of what they sell, there are other houses that put almost all merchandise in good condition before it goes on their block. All the brass and silver is polished; all mirrors

and picture glass replaced if broken; the rugs cleaned; the porcelain and glass washed; statuary repaired; lamps wired for American electrical systems; furniture refinished or even restored if merited. Such houses handle top quality goods and feel that their clientele will pay a high enough premium for mint condition merchandise to repay the considerable expense incurred in their preparation.

Most houses fall somewhere between either total perfection or absolute indifference, usually making some form of preparation. Rarely taking the time and expense necessary for major repairs, these houses will often clean or polish the better merchandise and may make minor repairs.

Preparations for Sale

After the auction house has made its choice as to the assembly of the auction and the attention that will be given the goods to be sold, it must decide in what order the sale will proceed. This is more important than it may appear, and a lot of psychology goes into this aspect of auctioneering. There are obviously many different routes open to the house. It may sell the merchandise in any order—whatever the floor man picks up or indicates will be sold. It may arrange the articles in a pattern that will create variety; three pieces of glass are followed by three pieces of furniture, which are followed by three pieces of porcelain. It may try to build the auction so that goods of lesser value are followed by goods of higher value, which are followed by goods of still higher value. It may group the merchandise so that all the glass is sold together, all the furniture together, all the porcelain together, and so forth. The aim of the arrangement, whether premeditated or not, is to maintain audience interest and to give everyone in the audience a chance to bid on something likely to interest him fairly early in the sale.

Houses that do not publish lists or catalogues for distribution to their customers have much more leeway in this matter. Even if the merchandise is numbered, the numbers may represent only identification for bookkeeping purposes and not be indicative of the order of the sale. The big advantage of this kind of flexibility is that, after beginning with ten or twelve articles of different kinds, the house is then free to put up in rapid succession whatever is selling well that day and to hold back articles of a kind not selling so well. In other words, houses that do not offer a published list quite often do not auction everything that is sitting or hanging about their hall.

Houses that publish lists usually intend to auction the merchandise in the order indicated by the list, so that they are locked into whatever order they chose at the time of making up the list. As a rule, the order will be something like this. The first few items will be of relatively low value or of little interest. This is because at the start of an average auction, many people have not taken their seats or have not entered into the swing of things. The crowd will still be noisy. After the first half dozen or so articles, things will begin to settle a bit, and somewhat more valuable merchandise will come up. From that point, the merchandise will be a mixture of values until about the last fifteen or so items from the end of the sale, when the values will again begin to diminish as the house anticipates a decrease in the audience. Throughout the sale, the house will have tried to maintain high audience interest by alternating all sorts of merchandise so that someone interested in furniture will not leave in a huff when he sees that items numbered 22 through 68 are nothing but small collectibles. A sample order, about one-quarter of the way through the sale, would be:

51. Framed simulated oil painting.
52. Umbrella stand.
53. Modern chest of drawers, walnut.
54. English porcelain vegetable dish.
55. Pair miniature porcelain jardinieres.
56. Wrought iron wall bracket.
57. Small spool day bed.
58. Pair mounted steer horns.
59. Spool turned corner chair.
60. Oak biscuit barrel.

Such a mix is not, of course, attempted or even considered desirable by some auction houses, which may prefer to use one of the alternate approaches. Not long ago I attended a sale where the order was the usual potpourri save for a large body of model railroad equipment, which was sold in the middle of the sale so that items 1 through 68 were miscellany, 69 through 107 railroad equipment, 108 through 200 miscellany. In this instance at least, this house felt that buyers of such equipment might not be interested in waiting through an entire sale to bid on what they had come for.

There is, I have heard, a successful auction operator in Pennsylvania who reserves the best two or three items of the sale until just a few minutes before the end, feeling that people who want the better merchandise will wait through the rest of the sale and possibly bid on other merchandise in the meantime.

The auction operator's decision about the order of sale should be based on his analysis of what will most interest the customers who patronize his establishment or conversely, as one operator pointed out, what will irritate them least. From the auctiongoer's point of view, there is probably no ideal approach to this problem unless it results in what he is interested in coming up first.

How helpful is a list or a catalogue to an audience? Some auctiongoers never consult lists or catalogues even when available; others feel uncomfortable without one. The auction house usually has some sort of list of merchandise to be sold or at least likely to be offered for sale during a given session, but the house faces the choice of whether or not to share this information with its customers. As mentioned, a list definitely limits the house's flexibility on merchandise to be offered, forcing it to rely on reserves if prices are unreasonably low.

Many auctiongoers and even non-auctiongoers collect catalogues and lists from auctions. Some dealers use the lists to note prices of all items sold and to base future buying decisions upon. Annotated auction lists over a period of years or even months can reveal interesting trends in buying patterns. As may be gathered, one of the advantages to the house of issuing lists or catalogues is that they serve as effective, continuing advertisements for the house.

The comprehensive catalogues of the big auction houses like Sotheby Parke-Bernet are avidly saved by private collectors and dealers because the kind of cataloguing done for an important sale offers invaluable aid to the individual who wants to reinforce his expertise. Authoritative cataloguing involves an expert or experts to authenticate the merchandise, a researcher to defend the judgment of authenticity, a writer to transmit this information, a photographer or artist to illustrate really significant pieces, an editor to put all this work in a usable format, and a printer to publish the catalogue.

Such ambitious projects are obviously beyond the financial capacity of most auction houses. Still, to the auctiongoer, even a simple list can be a big help. There are few things more frustrating than to sit through an entire dull auction waiting for one interesting piece, only to hear the auctioneer call, "That's all, folks," leaving your heart's desire unsold. Also, people attending unlisted sales will sooner or later have the experience of stepping outside for a minute and later finding that what they had been waiting for was sold while they were gone.

Whatever the advantages to the auctiongoer of a catalogue or list, the houses that do not issue them justify the omission by saying that either they do not get their merchandise in time to publish a list or the relatively small number of people who really depend on it does not justify the extra trouble and expense. Houses that offer lists often sell them for a nominal fee to cover the reproduction expense. Catalogues can cost as much as $5 or $10 each and are usually available in advance of big sales.

The question of display elicits as wide a range of opinions as that of cataloguing, both among auction operators and among auctiongoers. There are several schools of thought, regarding display. There is the "If they're really interested, they'll find what they're looking for" school. Here merchandise tends to be sorted generically and "display" consists of a pile of chairs next to a stack of tables next to a table overflowing with heaps of pottery next to a group of rolled up carpets. A step up from this super-casual approach is the practice of lining the furniture in rows so that auctiongoers can at least walk by the auctionables. Here, too, the smaller articles will be set on display shelves of some sort so that individual articles are visible to anyone caring to look. Most auction houses tend to favor this second approach, although on the occasion of a better sale, they may arrange the furniture in logical order. That is, a set of dining room furniture will be shown together and chairs will be reunited with the matching couch. Selected pieces of porcelain or glassware may be laid out on the tables or chests to be auctioned. Especially fine smaller articles, that might tempt sticky fingers at the pre-sale display, may be locked into lighted glass cases that serve both to highlight the merchandise's quality and to protect it. A

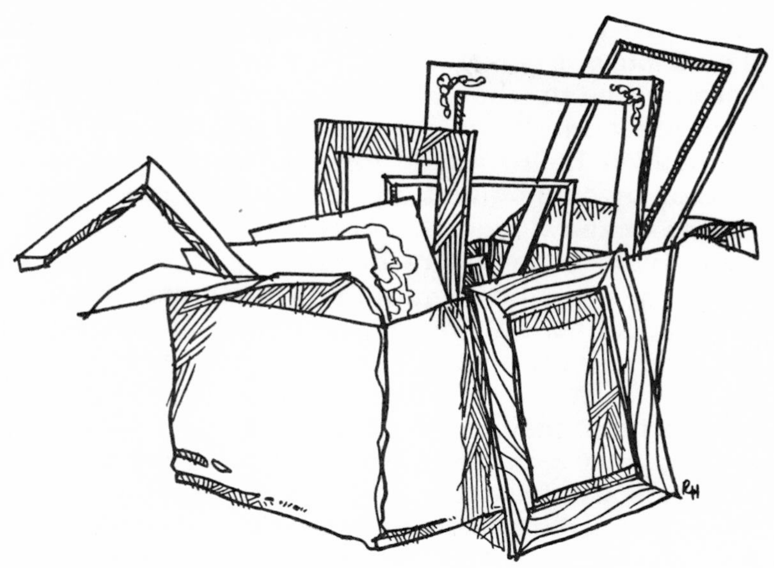

really ambitious auction house may go all out for an important sale to the extent of arranging the furniture in abbreviated room settings, down to the dinnerware on the dining room table and the flowers in the vase on the plant stand.

Few auction houses today attempt the sort of preparation made by Rose Lorenz at the American Art Association gallery at the end of the nineteenth century. Tyrannical Rose came into her own at the approach of a really important sale. The walls of the gallery would be redraped in the fabric and color most likely to enhance the works of art to be hung against them for pre-sale display, each valuable picture being carefully placed to take best advantage of the light. Hundreds of dollars worth of flowers would adorn the auction gallery on the fateful night. It must have been more like a Broadway opening for a new show than anything else.

Things are very different today. Even the auction house with the best intentions regarding display has problems that stem from the very nature of auctions. As one auctioneer apologized to a blue-ribbon crowd, "It's very different going into a store like Partridge's in London or Ginsburg &

Levy in New York where fine furniture is beautifully displayed and you can take your time to sit down and study it. Here we line up chairs on a plywood platform, but that's public auction. We do the best we can."

Whatever their attitude toward the importance or lack thereof of cataloguing and display, almost all auction houses acknowledge the necessity for advertising their sales. Word of mouth recommendation is admittedly the best form of advertising, but it is rarely enough because a lot of auctiongoers are selfish about their auction houses and tend to be closemouthed when they have found a good one.

Advertising may be as simple as placards nailed to trees or temporary signs stuck alongside the road. It may be as elaborate as a full-scale publicity campaign involving television and radio spots, as well as coverage in the trade and local press. Larger houses may advertise a big sale internationally. Most houses maintain a mailing list of good patrons and their particular preferences. Before special sales, cards will be sent to the people on the list or a member of the auction house staff will call the dealer or collector. He will advise that the upcoming sale will include the collectible in which the patron has expressed interest or simply that this is an especially good sale.

The advertising itself can be as straightforward as a mere statement of fact: there is to be an auction at a certain address handled by a certain auction house at a certain time. Or it may also include an abbreviated listing of merchandise to be sold or a description of the kind of merchandise to be sold. It may try for utter elegance: "Rarely in our many years of experience as this city's foremost auctioneers have we been privileged to offer such an exceptional sale to discriminating collectors." It may be down to earth: "We're having a real good auction, folks. A lot of good merchandise that you can afford to buy no matter who you are." It may be cutesy: "It takes a lot of nerve for us to advertise this sale. You've never seen such a funny looking bunch of stuff in your life. But if you don't have anything better to do Friday night, there might be something here that'll interest you."

Preparations for Sale

What will be sold, in what order, in what condition, with or without a published list, following what sort of display, under the auspices of what kind of advertising campaign are all questions that the auction house must answer before the sale can take place. The house must also decide which auctioneer (if it has more than one on its staff or on call) is best suited to conduct a particular sale. The time of the auction must be chosen and the day of the week.

Unless the house has only one auctioneer, the advantages and disadvantages that different auctioneers would bring to this particular sale must be weighed. Probable audience reaction to the auctioneer, his knowledge of the kind of merchandise to be sold, and his past record in handling such sales must be considered. As a general rule, you will notice that the higher the quality of the merchandise, the more dignified and knowledgeable the auctioneer. The wisecrack that makes fruit jars go like hotcakes on a cold morning may turn off the potential buyer of old Waterford.

There are many opinions about the best time of day to hold an auction. It is obviously self-defeating for a sale directed toward working men and women to be held on a weekday before six, yet so many people weekend out of town. If the sale is at night during the week, out-of-town auctiongoers may be discouraged. So go the arguments. As in so many other aspects of the auction business, there is no

ideal solution to the problem of time and day to hold an auction. Houses that do not auction regularly tend to hold their sales on weekends, while houses that stage regularly scheduled sales seem to prefer week nights.

Perhaps the best way of demonstrating the decision-making process facing the auction house is to trace a hypothetical consignment of merchandise from the time that it leaves its owners until it is sold by a medium-sized city auction house. This simplified account may help to reveal the pre-auction thought process.

Mr. and Mrs. Smith, an elderly couple and long-time collectors of old glass, are moving from a large house into a smaller apartment. They decide to sell part of their glass collection and feel that, in their area, an auction will be the most profitable way of doing this. They also wish to sell a few miscellaneous pieces of furniture and some house-hold fittings that they no longer need. When they call the local auction house, Brown's Galleries, let us say, an appraiser visits them to examine what they want to sell and to give his opinion of its market value and what it will bring at auction. Mr. and Mrs. Smith agree to let Brown's handle the sale for a commission of 20 percent, but stipulate reserve prices on many of the more valuable glass pieces and on one of the pieces of furniture. This means that Brown's must not sell these pieces for less than the reserve price designated by the Smiths.

The merchandise is crated and trucked to the auction house premises. There it is unpacked; and the staff lists it as having come from the Smiths, verifies its condition, and notes articles on which reserves have been placed. The consignment from the Smiths consists of:

108 pieces of old clear Moon & Star pattern glass (all mint condition)
1 primitive pine tavern table (good condition)
1 early nineteenth-century blanket chest (rough)
1 set of Melmac dinnerware (in original box)
1 11′5″ x 7′7″ Bokhara carpet (thin)
4 sets of green cotton satin drapes for picture windows (faded)

2 white Bates twin bedspreads, Queen Elizabeth pattern (one perfect, one badly stained)
1 large oak refectory table, 12′ long (good condition)
1 large Eastlake bookcase, 8′8″ tall (excellent condition except for small piece of molding on lower right side)
1 set complete works of Charles Dickens, simulated leather bindings (good conditon)
18 volumes of International Collectors Library series of classics, fancy bindings (like-new)
10 years of *National Geographic* (1955-1964)
4 assorted boxes of old magazines, mostly from 1960s

Except for reserve prices on most of the Moon & Star glassware and the oak refectory table, the merchandise is to be sold for whatever it will bring. Mr. Brown, operator and chief auctioneer of the house, who prides himself in overseeing every detail of his operation, must then make certain decisions about the merchandise.

He may handle it in several ways. His house has a regular auction of generally average quality every Friday night. Approximately every three or four months the house stages a sale of collectors' quality merchandise. About as often, a Saturday clearance auction is held to dispose of less interesting and valuable merchandise. Also, upon occasion, Brown's will assemble an auction featuring nothing but a certain kind of collectible item.

Thus, Mr. Brown may choose to include the Smith consignment as a block within an upcoming regular weekly auction, or he may distribute it among the several sorts of auctions put on by his house. He decides on the latter course.

Since the Moon & Star glassware is a uniquely large assortment and carries healthy though reasonable reserve prices, Mr. Brown decides to make it a prime attraction at his next special sale of collector's quality merchandise, which happens to be the disposal of the cream of the contents of a well-known Victorian mansion. He also decides to

include the Eastlake bookcase and the oak refectory table in this sale.

The collecting of primitives has grown in popularity in Mr. Brown's city, and he is accumulating merchandise of this sort until he has enough to stage a sale of all primitives. He designates the pine tavern table and the blanket chest to be included in this sale.

The oriental rug, the books, the unsoiled spread, and the *National Geographics* he marks for inclusion in the next regular auction. The remainder of the merchandise he designates for a clearance auction.

Thus, Mr. Brown chooses to distribute the Smiths' consignment so that it is likely to bring the maximum price that he feels it can attract at his house. This form of merchandising maximizes an individual item's potential by including it in an auction calculated to draw auctiongoers anticipating and ready to bid on items of this sort.

Preparations for Sale

Next Mr. Brown must determine to what extent the merchandise will be prepared for auction. Luckily, most of the Smith consignment is in good condition; and, at any rate, it is not the policy of Brown's Galleries to expend much effort in preparing merchandise. Thus, the Moon & Star glass will be washed if it has gotten dusty by auction time. The small strip of molding missing from the side of the Eastlake bookcase and found in a drawer will be glued in place. The soiled bedspread, however, will not be bleached. The blanket chest will not be tightened. Everything else will be sold "as is," save for dusting at the time the merchandise is displayed for auction.

Now that the merchandise consigned by the Smiths has been designated for certain sales and a decision has been made as to cleaning and minor repairs, we can look at the auction in which it will be sold.

Of the consignment, the first to be auctioned will be the oriental rug, the unsoiled bedspread, the books, and the several boxes of *National Geographic.* These items will be included in one of Brown's regular weekly sales. In these sales, Brown's offers a general assortment of merchandise ranging in quality from good to mediocre. Within the auction, the merchandise is arranged so that the sale begins with items of low value and little interest, progresses sporadically to items of greater value and interest, then slowly winds down to merchandise of less value at the auction's close. The arrangement is also designed to maintain a balance between porcelain, silver, furniture, glass, and other auctionables. Brown has found that such a mix maintains a high level of interest on the part of the people attending his sales.

Brown's does not catalogue any of its sales, but it provides lists for almost all sales, showing the order in which merchandise is to be sold. Often the list includes some qualifying or descriptive adjective. In an auction of 150 items, the Smiths' merchandise is listed thusly:

11. Bates bedspread (twin), Queen Elizabeth pattern.
30. 11′5″ x 7′7″ oriental rug, Bokhara, thin.

136. Set complete works Charles Dickens, simulated leather.
137. Eighteen volumes of classics, like new.
146. Choice of eight boxes of unbound *National Geographic* magazines, 1955-1964.

In the two-day, pre-sale display of the auctionables at Brown's Galleries, the bedspread is partially unfolded and hung over a large couch, another item to be auctioned. The rug is unfolded to lie flat on the floor in a corner of the display hall. The books are placed, their spines facing the audience, on shelves at the head of the hall. The boxes containing the National Geographics are stacked to one side of these shelves.

As usual, the weekly sale is advertised in the local newspaper, and a placard sits in the gallery's front window giving the time of the sale. The newspaper ad lists a few of the auction's more notable items and describes the remainder as "an interesting assortment." Auctiongoers reading this ad know what to expect even before attending the sale. It is plain that nothing of exceptional value is to be offered; neither will the sale be junky. Dealers and collectors attending the sale are not likely to feel disappointed. Of the several auctioneers available to him, Mr. Brown chooses one who has a pleasant, low-key manner in handling merchandise of average quality and who is known for getting higher than usual prices for merchandise of this kind.

At the sale, the auctioneer describes the Bates spread as "one of the finest spreads you can buy, and they never wear out." The spread goes for $20. Of the Bokhara, he says, "It has good color, and it's usable." The rug gets $185. Of the set of Dickens, he says, "No child should grow up without 'A Christmas Carol' in the house, and look at everything else you get besides. Look nice sitting on your bookshelves." The books bring $18. He looks at the fancy bindings of the Collectors Library books and whistles, "With these, you won't need anything else on your shelves." The books bring a hefty $2.25 each, for a total of $31.70. of the *Geographics,* almost at the end of the sale, he claims, "A lot of people are collecting these. They never go out of date. Great if you have students in your family, and these are in new condition.'' The *Geographics* sell for an average price of $9 per box.

At the sale's end, $326.70 (less the house's commission of 20 percent) is credited to the Smith consignment account. As usual, the merchandise did not sell exactly as expected. The appraiser was disappointed that the rug, for example, did not bring more, but the other articles brought at least what he had estimated.

The next auction including any of the Smith merchandise is the sale of the contents of the Victorian mansion. As Mr. Brown had envisioned, the Moon & Star glass and the oak refectory table and Eastlake bookcase make excellent additions to this sale. Most of the items to be sold are high-quality Victorian furniture and accessories in good condition. Within the sale, the Moon & Star glass is scattered in groups of three or four, the furniture as follows:

21. Large oak refectory table (12′ long), excellent condition.

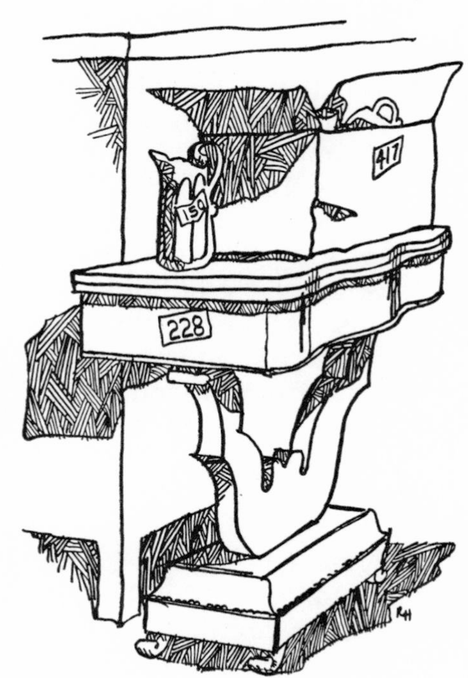

36. Large Eastlake bookcase (8′8″ tall), exellent condition.

As this is a relatively important sale for his house, Mr. Brown has taken more pains than usual with both display and advertising. The merchandise is arranged more carefully. The Moon & Star glass is arranged in a display case and lit. For this sale, Brown advertises in advance in trade papers, describing it as: "A collection of superb Victorian furniture and accessories from a famous Victorian home. Also, large collection of antique Moon & Star glassware." The week of the sale, advertising is run in the local press in the usual manner, but the wording emphasizes the high quality of the merchandise to be offered. Handbills are distributed at shops offering Victoriana or collectors' glassware. Brown's assistant calls collectors and dealers on the house's mailing list and advises them that they will not want to miss this exceptional auction.

Mr. Brown himself will be the auctioneer, as this sale will draw a select audience expecting informed presentation of the merchandise.

At the sale, Mr. Brown describes the table as "an unusually large and well decorated example of English Victorian furniture in the Jacobean style. Probably dates from the 1870s." The table has a reserve price of $150. When Mr. Brown cannot start it for any sum near that figure, he passes it. He says that the bookcase is "a handsome example of late Eastlake, 1880 or so, with the typical gallery around the top. Very fine walnut veneer on the side panels. The glass is intact." The bookcase sells for $125. The Moon & Star glass, scattered throughout the sale, elicits spirited bidding without any particular urging from Mr. Brown; the total amount realized by it is $2,560. Obviously the gallery's advertising has attracted several serious glass collectors eager to add to their collections.

At the end of the sale $2,685 (less 20 percent) is credited to the Smiths' consignment account. The bookcase sold for the appraiser's estimate. The table was a disappointment and is held for a later sale, but the glassware realized almost 30 percent more than the appraiser had predicted.

A few weeks later is the primitives auction where the Smiths' pine trestle table and early blanket chest will be sold. This sale is advertised on several spots on a youth-oriented radio station, also by handbills distributed to shops catering to youthful apartment dwellers. As anticipated, the crowd is overwhelmingly under thirty and of the sort that decorating magazines like to feature. Prices are good, and the table brings $30 and the chest $50. Another $80 is credited to the Smiths' account.

The remainder of the Smith consignment is sold at a weekend clearance auction. Brown's holds these auctions every few months on a weekend. Here there is no list. Display consists simply of casual piles of merchandise through which auctiongoers poke at will. Advertising is a two-line insertion in the local papers announcing: "Auction! Odds and ends clearance sale. Many bargains. 1 P.M. Saturday." The auctioneer is earthy, an eagerly friendly fellow. Of the Smiths' drapes, he remarks, "Sure they're a little worn, but they'll still keep the neighbors from seeing what you're up to." The drapes bring $6 for the lot; the magazines $5; the new Melmac $3; and the soiled Bates spread ("It may bleach out; take a chance") $8. At this sale's end, $22 more is credited to the Smiths' account.

Thus, after several auctions and almost as many months, the Smith consignment is disposed of for a figure slightly in excess of the appraiser's estimates. It may be that the Smiths' merchandise would have brought about the same amount of money at any given sale, but it is much more likely that Brown's careful placement of the merchandise increased the sale price (and the amount of Brown's commission) and also benefited the customer who came looking generally for what he found and bought.

This hypothetical consignment will give you an idea of the thought and preparations that must precede most auctions. In each instance, circumstances permitting, the clever auction house will sell a consignment or acquisition as part of the auction where it should bring the best price. Perhaps this should be the credo of every auction house: "To sell the merchandise to the people who want it enough to pay the best price."

Chapter 6

The Auctiongoer

Now we all know who goes to auctions. The little old lady in tennis shoes who nosily watches what everybody else is doing when she isn't compulsively buying old Mason jars. Right? And the wealthy dilettante who buys anything that catches his fancy regardless of cost? And, of course, the wily dealers who somehow manage to get all of the "good stuff"? Right again.

According to popular fancy, these are the bulk of auctiongoers. Anyone else has just wandered in by mistake.

Maybe this was true way back when, although I rather doubt it. It certainly is not today. Oh, an occasional pair of tennis shoes may be seen, but the majority of today's auctiongoers bear little resemblance to any of the long-held, quirky stereotypes.

So who does go to auctions?

It varies from sale to sale. Obviously, a sale of primitives will bring out a different sort of crowd than a sale of the contents of a movie star's house. The couples who paid $8 to attend the auction of the showy if rag-tag end of the

Anna Thomson Dodge estate in 1972 will probably not be sitting next to you when Joe's Auction Emporium puts up rusty farm bells tonight.

Still, it is possible, by personal observation and through the surveying of auctiongoers at fairly typical sales (that is, sales where the most expensive item is unlikely to break anyone's budget, but where no actual junk is sold), to determine something of the makeup of today's typical auctiongoer.

Keeping in mind that averages may be misleading, here is our average auctiongoer. He or she (for there seems to be no particular pattern as to sex) is approximately forty-five years of age and has been attending auctions between five and ten years. The odds are fifty-fifty that he will have a business connection with the antiques, used furniture, or gift shop trade. If he is not always a dealer, neither is he always a dedicated collector; most auctiongoers buy whatever suits their fancy, their fancy encompassing an extremely catholic range. He is usually well, if casually, dressed and has at least a high school education and often some college. He probably has a slightly better than average income. Whenever possible he attends an auction once or twice a week.

Yet, if this is our average auctiongoer, he is joined at almost every sale by teenagers and retirees ready to bid with equal zeal against him. There will be people present who have never before been to an auction and people who have been going for thirty years. There will be some people of very limited means, and even one or two who could probably write a check for the entire evening's sales. Still, our average auctiongoer is fairly typical of those who attend a majority of auctions.

Every man or unusual man, why do auctiongoers go? There are basically seven kinds of auctiongoers: the dealer in antiques; the gift shop operator; the dealer in junk furniture; the interior decorator; the collector; the auction hound; and the accidental attendant. Each kind of auctiongoer has his own reasons.

Dealers, in popular non-dealer folklore, are the villains of the piece. It is they who bid up the really good stuff, they who intimidate the amateur, they who carry off the best of the spoils.

Do dealers always get all the "good stuff"? It is highly unlikely that they even get most of it, provided that there are knowledgeable private collectors in the audience. The reason is simple. The dealer must be able to buy at a price low enough so that he can make a 20 to 50 percent profit. He is, after all, a businessman. The collector, on the other hand, can afford to pay whatever his purse will allow for whatever he wants. Dealers can take it all only when the other auctiongoers at a particular sale do not know values and are afraid to bid on anything but junk that is going cheap. And one can hardly expect the dealer, delighted at getting a chest worth $400 retail for $150 at auction, to forebear and let that sweet little housewife have it for $140.

Occasionally, dealers can bid up to their heart's content, at least to a certain point, whatever the object's value. These are the professionals bidding for a client who has commissioned them to get a certain item.

Some dealers go to auctions for a reason that is both illegal and reprehensible: the infamous dealer rings, a device for eliminating costly competitive bidding. In the operation of the ring, certain dealers at a sale agree in advance not to bid against each other on some items so that a representative of the ring can buy the merchandise for much less than would be possible if other ring members competed with him. At the end of the sale, the ring holds its own miniature auction, with the highest bidders getting the different items bought by the ring representative. The difference between the acutal auction cost of each item and the amount bid at the ring auction is divided among the ring members.

The ring has advantages not only for the dealers actually wanting the merchandise, but also for the hangers-on. In the opinion of one long-time auctioneer, three-quarters of the dealers in a ring are there only to collect the money that they will make from the operation of the ring. Out of twenty dealers in a hypothetical ring, perhaps only two or three are genuinely interested in a specific item; the others are simply picking up loose change, collecting pay for attending the auction and going along with their fellows.

Basically, however, most dealers who attend auctions do so in the hope of buying merchandise at a price low enough so that the regulation markup (which varies from area to area and from dealer to dealer) is possible for resale.

Not all people attending auctions from motives of business are dealers per se. Flea marketers, that ubiquitous breed who descend upon the disused meadows and abandoned drive-in movie lots of America in the spring, go to buy anything fairly small that is going very cheap. Decorators, clients often in tow, go to find that unusual something to complete their latest project. Museums buy to complete their collections.

Serious private collectors also go to auction to add to their collections, whose content naturally dictates which auctions they attend. A collector of Georgian glass would waste time attending a sale of plants. Many collectors, however, do not consider the auction a good hunting ground for medium quality merchandise. Prices, they say, are too high, due primarily to non-collectors bidding up something just because it is "pretty," having no idea of its real value.

Auction hounds go to auction to buy anything that they

like and even something that they never knew that they liked until they saw that it was going low. Auction hounds who degenerate into addicts are likely to buy anything when the mood is upon them. They become as fascinated with the machinery and the mood of the auction as with the merchandise that it offers.

Then, believe it or not, there are some people who apparently go to auctions out of habit. They rarely buy anything; and when they do, the purchase is only incidental. These carefree souls go to auctions as other mortals brush their teeth—more from routine than any conscious thought process involving motivation. The auction is there; therefore, they go. It is this group that produces the peripheral loungers who stand on the sidelines and make cryptic comments, who laugh loudest at the auctioneer's hoariest jokes, and even louder at his mistakes.

A lot of people who go to auctions, dealers and collectors alike, do so at least in part to meet other people, to keep up with what is going on in that tight little world that interests them so much—the world of dusty shops crammed with bric-a-brac and Empire furniture, the world in which the future of depression glass is considered with as much gravity as others view the future of the dollar.

Most people go to auctions expecting to find real bargains, while others see the sale mainly—as one auctiongoer put it—"as a kind of side show." In this latter category, one would have to put the morbidly curious who always seem to turn out in droves whenever the estate of a murder victim goes up, as well as the nosy Parkers who poke gleefully through the linens and crockery of the last of a well-known family.

Another auctiongoer confessed that for her the sale represents a ceaseless flow of fascinating merchandise, mostly from an earlier, less complicated time. To her, a Windsor chair on the block is not only a usable object, but also a tangible link to the people who so lovingly made and used it in some long ago time and place. These long forgotten people, thus, become in a sense her "personal friends."

Since the main purpose in the holding of an auction is to exchange merchandise for money, it is interesting to see just how much money most auctiongoers part with. A survey of typical auctiongoers reveals that auctions are not the hangout of the last of the big spenders. When asked what was the highest price they'd paid for one item at auction, those surveyed gave sums averaging $345. When asked what was the most that they had ever spent at any one auction, the average was $790. When asked what they spent at the average auction, the answer was $410. This averaging process applied both to dealers and collectors. When only the answers of the non-dealers were averaged, a much more modest result developed: $210 for the single highest priced item; $325 for the auction at which the most was spent; and, most significant, less than $100 at the average auction.

As is usual when people spend money, there are as many approaches as there are people. One school holds firmly to the absolute necessity, for example, of careful, pre-sale examination of the merchandise. Over 80 percent of the dealers and 90 percent of the non-dealers surveyed stressed the importance of the preview. Quite a few regular auctiongoers, in fact, emphasized that neither expert nor novice should pass up an examination of the merchandise if it is at all possible.

Confirming this basically cautious approach is the fact that of the auctiongoers queried, over 50 percent of the non-dealers and almost 30 percent of the dealers stated that they attended an auction to bid only on one or more items that they had examined and chosen in advance of the sale.

There are, of course, other auctiongoers who rarely if ever do more than glance at the merchandise on their way to their seats. They buy as the old time pilots used to fly—by the seat of their pants.

Different methods of bidding also have their devotees. There is the voice aproach—"Here!"—loud and to the point if somewhat obvious. There is the hesitant wave, the tentative nod, the flickering handkerchief. There is the businesslike display of the registration card or paddle. And there are a variety of abrupt hand motions, perhaps the most common being the sideways chop, which necessitates the bidder's sitting or standing in relative isolation for obvious reasons. Few people at the average contemporary auction bid by prearranged signal.

As methods of bidding differ, so do approaches to timing. This stems from diametrical philosophies as much as anything else. One man told me, "If you bid too fast, the auctioneer will see that you're eager and bid you up." His companion agreed, "I like to hesitate—just for a second or

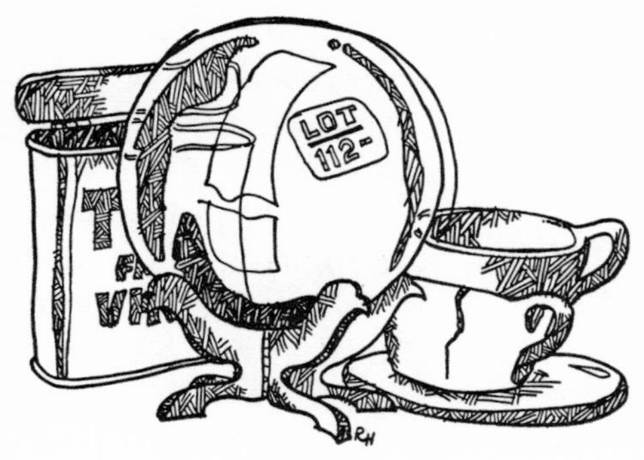

two—to show 'em I'm really thinking about it. It won't hurt 'em to wonder a little.'' One woman interviewed, a dealer and collector, noted her disapproval of this approach: ''If you know what something's worth to you, then there's no point in fooling around with your bidding. While you're playing cute, the auctioneer may just get disgusted and knock the item down to someone else.''

Some auctiongoers will not open bidding on any item. Others will advance only in units suggested by the auctioneer; still others try to halve or third the requested advance.

Bidding is used aggressively by some auctiongoers, the bane of the auctioneer's life. These are the people who, when the auctioneer has $35 and is trying for $45, will bid $42.60, usually quite loudly. Then, there are also the jump bidders, the ones who arrogantly yell, ''$200'', when the auctioneer is trying to advance from $150 to $175. These tactics are designed to intimidate the other bidders by making them think that there is no point in bidding against this determined person. Another effort at confusing the competition is backing up on bids rather than advancing; offering $20 when the auctioneer has $25 bid and is trying to get $30. Auctioneers save a special dislike for such clever types, for they break the rhythm of the sale and distract or even disturb other auctiongoers.

Among auctiongoers there is a lot of talk about buying philosophies and how successful auctiongoers have a philosophy which they follow consistently. Several people said that nobody ever opens bidding on an item at the first price suggested by the auctioneer. Others said that everybody who knew what they were doing never bid past that amount, no matter what the bidding started at; if the auctioneer tried to start a vase for $10, then managed to get a $2 start, only a novice would bid beyond the $10 point. Still others claimed that you could bid up to twice what the auctioneer suggested as the opening bid and come out O.K. (The effectiveness of these ideas as guides to true value depends, as we have already seen, on the auctioneer.)

I heard many other things as well, but the gist of most of them was that everyone who goes to auctions regularly has a buying philosophy that is tied to the auctioneer's suggested opening bid. Do the facts bear out this claim? Are experienced auctiongoers so consistent in their approach to bidding?

At a dozen fairly typical auctions, I noted the auctioneer's suggested opening bid, the actual opening bid, the successful bid, and the name or number of the auctiongoer who triumphed. Analysis of these figures suggests that while people may talk a lot about theories, when it comes to the auction, theories tend to be forgotten.

If experienced auctiongoers (and the bulk of the successful bidders at the auctions in question did not appear to be novices) held to any such theory or theories, then a pattern should emerge from the statistics. And the pattern just isn't there. Time after time the same person had successful bids on items that sold not only at a price below the suggested opening bid, but also considerably in excess of it. Several of the same people who had assured me so confidently that they never exceeded the suggested opening bid were among those fighting for the privilege on items that particularly interested them.

Another common belief is that at almost every auction two or three people buy almost everything; and to be honest, it often sounds that way. At the first few auctions I attended, it seemed that item after item would go to No. 11 or No. 84 or whatever the predominant number or numbers happened to be.

But the figures don't bear this out. While it is true that there will usually be at least one or two auctiongoers who will buy more articles than the average auctiongoer at the sale, it is equally true that it is unusual for any one or two or even three auctiongoers to walk away overwhelmingly successful bidders. Rather, the statistics indicate that the majority of the items in any given sale go to auctiongoers who buy only this one thing or possibly two things at most.

Another fallacy that suffers from the figures is, "Oh no, she's here, and she always buys all the glass." It is true that on occasion one collector, determined to have a big night of it, will buy all the glass, but this is not the norm. It is a rare sale when one bidder walks off with all the glass or clocks or porcelain or all of anything.

My admittedly limited samples also show that few bidders stick to just one sort of item. That is, it is an unusual auctiongoer who walks away from the sale with only furniture or artwork or rugs. If the auctiongoer has bought several items, a preference for a certain sort of item may emerge, but that is all. By my figures, most auctiongoers who bought more than three items bought at least two different kinds of merchandise.

Still, admitting the truth of this demonstrated universality in buying, most auctiongoers do have decided preferences before they walk into the auction. Before beginning the statistical studies for this book, I would have said that more people collect porcelain than anything else—at least in the area where I do most of my regular auctiongoing. (That, of course, is because I am a blue and white addict myself and sometimes feel as if I am fending off a veritable horde of competition whenever anything remotely like old Staffordshire comes up.) Survey results, however, indicated otherwise.

Keeping in mind that many auctiongoers collect more than one kind of item, I found that, of the auctiongoers questioned, 55 percent collect furniture, 38 percent glass, 26 percent porcelain, 17 percent silver, 12 percent artwork, 12 percent books, 2 percent statuary. Also, 26 percent collect miscellany ranging from primitive hand tools to old barometers to jade, while 12 percent claim that they collect nothing per se, but simply buy whatever appeals to them.

When I asked one prominent auctioneer about the buying patterns of his customers, he snorted, "They may or may not buy almost anything; it depends on the crowd. But one thing I do know; I don't believe that a lot of people who go to auctions know quality. I never cease to be amazed at what junk will bring when people are ignoring good stuff."

What do people do with the things that they buy? If they are dealers, they usually sell auction finds either in their own establishments or through the shops of others. Some dealers also have private collections and keep part of what they buy for their own use. Auctiongoers who characterize themselves as collectors usually keep their auction spoils for personal use. Some people use them as gifts for friends and relatives.

Some people simply hoard what they buy at auction. An auction operator said of a particularly acquisitive patron: "There's an old man over here who got his big old country house so full of stuff that he had to buy himself a trailer and move out of his house. It wasn't long 'til he got the trailer full, and he bought another trailer. Now it's almost full, and I guess when that happens, he'll just buy another one."

Most people who go to auctions are quite voluble in their appraisal of them. While a few say, "The ones I attend are fine," most auctiongoers seem less content with the auction process. The complaints fall into four basic categories: material, economic, psychological, and physical.

Several auctiongoers described the general quality of most of the merchandise now going on the block at the average auction as inferior. They said that auction houses,

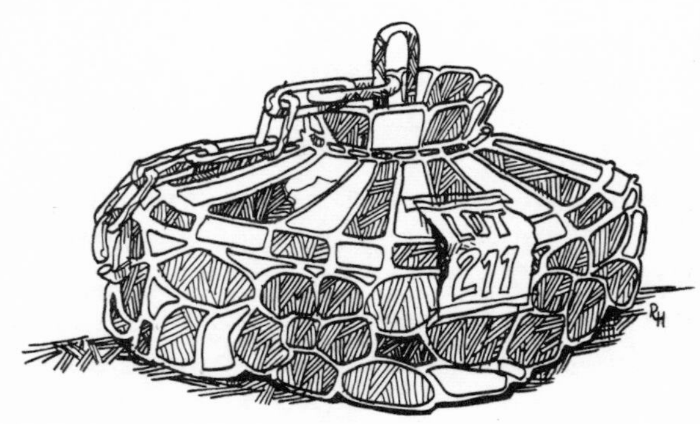

most of which also operate retail shops on the side, are reluctant to put the best of their consignments in auctions, feeling that they can get higher prices selling retail or even wholesale.

The single most irritating thing cited by most of the experienced auctiongoers was what one regular described as: "the continual misrepresentation of merchandise." There were different opinions from the complainers as to the reason for the misrepresentation. More charitable souls tended to think that the auctioneers really do not know the merchandise that they sell and that their mistakes are inadvertent. Cynics, the vast majority, felt that the misrepresentation is quite deliberate, the degree of it geared to how much the auctioneer thinks a particular crowd will swallow. One woman complained that not only do the auctioneers in her area lie to the auctiongoers about the merchandise, but also they are tactless enough to laugh when they put an especially good one over.

Another fairly common complaint was that it is almost impossible to get real bargains any more, that the house will bid against you even if no one else will. As one dealer put it, "Auctions are where you get stung. I prefer estate sales. At least there you know where you are."

The psychological side of auctiongoing disturbed a few regulars. "If you want to get a certain kind of merchandise at a reasonable price," said one dealer, "then you have to go to auction, but I don't like it. It's too emotional. It's hard to make a sensible buying decision in that kind of atmosphere."

The greatest number of complaints dealt with the physical arrangements of most auctions. It seems that there is very little here that suits most auctiongoers, many of whom had more than one gripe. Fully 45 percent of the auctiongoers questioned complained of the lack of adequate temperature control in the indoor auctions. Inadequate display techniques, both before and during the sale, bothered 44 percent of those surveyed. Over 43 percent protested the lack of comfortable seating. Poor lighting of the merchandise was mentioned by 36 percent. Almost 30 percent didn't think the acoustics were good enough. A failure to catalogue or list the merchandise was cited by nearly 20 percent. The fact that most auction houses do not offer delivery bothered another 20 percent. The lack of easily available refreshments was noted by 13 percent, and 10 percent thought that payment procedures could be more efficient.

As a defense, the auction houses can point to the remark of one old hand as typical of the feelings of the majority: "I don't go to be comfortable or to eat. I go to buy." A seconding voice protested: "After all, it isn't the theatre, and too much comfort brings those who come only for fun."

Uncomfortable or not, auctions do draw at least some people strictly out for fun. In some rural areas, in fact, going down to the auction barn of a Saturday night to watch the city slickers throw away their money is a popular local pastime. As Pendleton-clad ladies compete furiously for old pattern glass, the locals line the walls, swigging soda and crunching popcorn, only occasionally hooting when something especially outrageous pierces their bucolic calm.

There is often as much amusement in watching the audience as there is in watching the auctioneer; eavesdropping is easy, in fact usually impossible to avoid. Of course, one occasionally hears comments perhaps best left out of wholesome books such as this (it is amazing how many physical objects lend themselves to scatalogical commentary); but on the whole, the remarks are rarely more than cutting.

It is fun to see the auctiongoers get their own back, and an amateur Don Rickles league seems to exist at almost every sale. Like the gum-chewing, overalls-clad man who sat quietly while a fast talking auctioneer extolled the virtues of a particularly bad oil painting—a gross, sickly white bust of some Roman emperor suffering from acute dyspepsia depicted against a muddy red curtain, obviously the work of a first year art student with no future in his craft. When no one would give him even a $10 start on the unframed canvas, the auctioneer groaned, "You see before you what is possibly the finest painting you will see in a long time. A great work of art. Now what do you say to that?" Packing his cud in one side of his cheek, the man drawled, "I say you're goin' to hell if you keep on tellin' such lies as that."

The man sitting next to me watched a set of 1920s, not very good dining room furniture go up. Its finish was more alligator than otherwise; its color was indeterminate; and its general proportions squatty. The only distinctive thing about it was that it had ball-and-claw feet. The auctioneer took one look at those feet and bawled, "A fine set of furniture. Chippendale, you can tell by the feet." To which impulsive description, my man snickered, "Yeah, Fred Chippen Dale."

One woman bought several pieces of rather good furniture, all of them French polished to within an inch of losing their American citizenship. Immediately following them—the result of poor placement on somebody's part—was a pathetic, turn-of-the-century chest whose veneer was trying to warp and whose color resembled nothing so much as a cup of coffee left to form mold. As the auctioneer looked at it, trying desperately to think of something to say in its favor, the French polish freak yelled out, "Just say it's Polish polished, Mack." At which point a good-looking Polish-American in the front row threatened to sue for slander.

Of course, a lot of the activity has nothing to do with auctions. One night the man behind me was describing in normal conversational tones what he told his wife when she found out that he and his secretary weren't really working late that night. Then there's the woman who takes thirty minutes to explain why Harry couldn't make it that night—the explanation directed toward a man three rows back.

It sometimes seems that people come to auctions for the express purpose of eating. Perhaps it is due to the nervousness engendered by desire and frustration, but many auctions have a crumb fallout large enough to feed an army of mice. And people are not picky; whatever is available is what they will eat. Elegant buffet dinner or stale Twinkies are gulped with exactly the same glassy-eyed determination. Domestic champagne or vintage Coke satisfy the same thirst. The eating starts before the auction begins and continues until the last stragglers leave. One wag suggested that the appropriate theme song for the auction would be, "Crunch, crunch, crunch, the folks are eating, as their bids they are a-bleating." The man next to him then confiscated his moon pie and Pepsi Cola as punishment.

By and large, auctiongoers are nice folks (except for those who smoke in no-smoking areas, show up drunk and noisy, bring along screaming babies, or—most of all—outbid you on something you really want). There's nothing really peculiar about auctiongoers. I mean, a lot of people who don't go to auctions have an elephant foot wastebasket, don't they? The average auctiongoer is like someone you might know; in fact, he probably is.

In summation, a wide variety of people attend auctions for many reasons. Some of them don't like auctions all that much; others find the auctioneer's cadence more soothing than a Gregorian chant. There's only one thing most auctiongoers agree on: they find something at auctions that keeps them coming back.

Chapter 7

The Auction

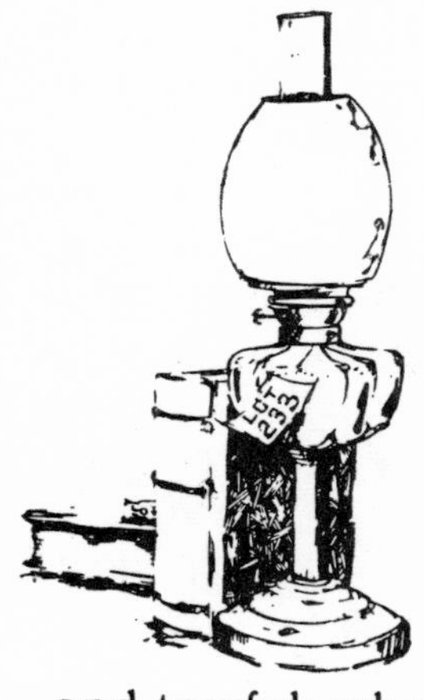

William Makepeace Thackery writes in *Vanity Fair* of auctions:

> If there is any exhibition in all Vanity Fair which Satire and Sentiment can visit arm-in-arm together; where you light on the strangest contrasts laughable and tearful: where you may be gentle and pathetic, or savage and cynical, with perfect propriety: it is at one of those public assemblies.

Human interest abounds at auctions. It could not be otherwise. What once belonged here will now go there, and at times we cannot help wondering about the reason for the transfer. It is a tribute to the effective diversionary tactics of the auction process that this sort of mood so rarely strikes even the most inveterate auctiongoer.

This is as it should be, for the auction is essentially just a mechanism for the efficient merchandising of physical objects. To try to read into it a microcosm of the ultimate fate of all objects—and humans—is to probe Wordsworthian "thoughts that do often lie too deep for tears."

In any event, at this point it is not the philosophy of auctions that concerns us, but rather their mechanics. In a nuts-and-bolts approach, we will look at what you may expect when you go to auction in the way of physical facilities, conduct of the sale, and the role that you must play if you plan to bid.

To begin with the obvious, every auction must be held somewhere. Contrary to the impression given by old movies like Hitchcock's *North by Northwest,* most auctions are not held in elegantly furnished salons. They are, in fact, held almost any place where it is possible for people to gather in numbers larger than a dozen. Auctions are held in tents, open meadows, deconsecrated churches, old army barracks, storage warehouses, post offices, motels, and private houses, as well as in the usual gallery auditorium.

I recall a country auction held in a prefabricated building that looked as if a good wind might end its selling days. The floor was uncovered plywood sheets, the walls warped pseudo-wood paneling. The ceiling was nothing more than unfinished, exposed wooden rafters, from which square floor fans had been suspended at intervals to stir the sluggish air. Round black metal posts supported the ceiling. Door openings were covered by large pieces of corrugated metal cut to fit, and the auctioneer's podium was made of the same paneling that covered the walls. A surprisingly comfortable note was provided by heavily padded theatre seats. By the large back entrance to the auction area stood two coin machines dispensing soft drinks and peanut butter crackers. The haze of cigarette and cigar smoke was so thick that the naked light bulbs hanging from the ceiling did not shine, but glowed as in a fog. From the back of the room, the auctioneer—a typical tobacco-style auctioneer sporting a colonel's hat symbolic of his calling and holding the microphone close to his lips in a curiously suggestive fashion—was hardly visible. Customers wandered about in the hazy light, peering at rows of Victorian hat racks and beds, looking at the marks on turn-of-the-century European porcelain, and surreptitiously thumping old milk cans.

The Auction

Many of the customers were of retirement age; the hall was crowded; and in an effort at compensation, the operator of the auction house turned the P.A. system to a pitch that made one's ears ring nearly as long as one's eyes smarted after leaving the auction.

Quite different in feel was an auction in an old church.

Considering that it is a secondary, unplanned-for usage, auctions fare well in church buildings. There is plenty of room for merchandise display. The churches were built originally for reasonably large assemblies of people to congregate in decent comfort for a period of time. Also, the acoustics are generally good and the buildings sound. Our forefathers did not grudge the Lord's house its fair portion of sturdiness. Granting all this and the fact that some use must be made of deconsecrated church buildings, it is nonetheless piquant to go through the double doors of what—even if I had not seen the building's exterior and the neatly fenced graveyard—I would recognize as an old Methodist church, cousin to the one that I attended as a child when I visited my grandparents in the country.

At this particular sale, the pews had been replaced by comfortable, padded folding chairs. In place of a minister's pulpit, there was a high desk at which the auctioneer and his clerk sat. The area behind, once the choir, was stacked high with junk furniture. Only one reminder, apart from the unmistakable shape of the building itself, remained of the original use: on the wall to the rear and left side of the choir was the wooden framed board used to post the numbers of the hymns for the service. Now the numbers in bright red DayGlo stated the time of the next sale.

As would have been the case at church, small clusters of obviously acquainted people hovered at various points around the building, laughing and chattering, while determined looking, sharp-eyed men scanned the crowd and the merchandise. Dress was casual. Children ran about, upsetting chairs. At the start of the sale, the fast-talking, youthful auctioneer reminded the nosiy audience that coffee and doughnuts were available in the rear, and motioned to already sweaty, khaki-clad young helpers to bring up the first lot.

In marked contrast was the small, but elegant, city gallery, on whose green onyx floor subtly colored carpets formed a rich pattern. Restored oils hung in dark corners. Potential bidders were registered in a red leather-bound book, then offered refreshment. The podium was mirrored; the auctioneer sat on a Chippendalish side chair with especially vigorous ball and claw feet. Chandeliers glittered discreetly overhead, hung from a ceiling thick with plaster acanthus leaves. There was no more than a low murmur of talk and occasional laughter as the stylishly dressed crowd drifted through antique-lined corridors and took their seats on small folding chairs in the main salesroom. Many people sipped champagne as the auctioneer introduced the staff —the attractive young men and women (in evening dress) who showed the merchandise—and stipulated the terms of sale. The auctioneer himself was young, with the calm, assured elegance of a youthful Leslie Howard. His approach was low-key, even offhanded, but knowledgeable. The whole proceeding, in fact, was so quiet and restrained that it came as a distinct shock to leave the gallery's reception area and find traffic streaming noisily by on one of the city's busiest streets.

The variations in setting are infinite, but the point is that auctions may pop up almost anywhere (and usually in buildings or open spaces with anything but this in mind) so that the determined auctiongoer may at times meet some discomfort in the pursuit of the hobby.

If the sale is to be held in a city gallery, you can, at an average auction, at least be sure of a seat. Otherwise, unless you know the conditions under which a sale will be held, it is best to be prepared for the worst in the way of weather and seating. You will never realize more poignantly the worth of an umbrella than when you are the only person holding one as the heavens open and the rains begin to fall on the back meadow where you and fifty other people have gathered to bid on old wicker. And, if you frequent a lot of country sales, you'll be glad you purchased that old folding camp stool. Although almost all auctions will provide some seating, even if out of doors, few provide enough for the crowds that show up. That stool may turn an impossible experience into a profitable afternoon.

A final caution regarding the physical arrangements of auctions: do not assume that the temperature at any auction will approximate ideal climate control. In plainer terms, you will probably be hot in summer, cold in winter,

so dress accordingly. Layers work well; sweaters, scarves, and gloves can be added or shed as the temperature demands.

Now, what should you expect once you've decided to go to an interesting-sounding auction advertised in the classified section of the daily newspaper?

As you walk into the hall or area where the auction is to be held, there will usually be someone sitting at a desk registering people who plan to bid. If you think there is even the slightest chance that you might bid, you should stop here and register. As a rule, all that is required in registration is your name, address, and phone number; and, upon furnishing these, you will be assigned a bidding number and often given a card or paddle on which the number is printed or written. At rare auctions, you may be asked to furnish further information; and you should not take this amiss unless the questions are inapplicable.

In fact, if you are strange to an auction house, especially if it is located in any other than your home town, and you think it possible that you may be doing a considerable amount of purchasing at the sale, then it is probably sensible after registering to seek out the auctioneer or auction operator, identify yourself, and offer references if requested. This small precaution forestalls the moment —about halfway through the sale at an unfamiliar house where you have been buying big—when a pleasant but determined member of the auction house's staff sidles into the seat next to yours and begins to draw you out apologetically but firmly. It's hard to blame the house because strangers have been known to swoop down, buy everything in sight, load it into their station wagons, then pay for the whole lot with a bad check.

It is at the registration desk that you will find the catalogue or list of the merchandise to be sold, if one has been prepared for public distribution. A catalogue of any size with illustrations and a slick or even hard cover may cost you anywhere from fifty cents to several dollars. Lists are usually either given away or sold for a nominal amount. For the auction itself, there is rarely any admission charge. Only at sales where the house anticipates a turnout in excess of the house's capacity will you have to pay an admission fee. By charging admission (which is generally credited against any purchase), the house hopes to discourage mere lookers to save room for people seriously interested in buying. Another sort of auction for which there is often an admission charge is that staged for the benefit of some civic or social group. Here, the charge is usually treated as a contribution to the cause for which the sale is being held.

Having registered and received your list of merchandise or catalogue, you now stand inside the hall or sale area. If the sale has not begun, you may wander about the area where the merchandise is arranged.

If the human as well as the material side of auctions interests you, you will enjoy pre-sale inspection. This is when family discussions reveal that he thinks those mounted antlers are worth $25 and she thinks he ought to have his head examined. It is during this pre-sale display that you get to meet people—dealers and collectors, as well as interested and often interesting onlookers. Many auctiongoers are friendly folk; and if you take with a grain of salt much of what they say about the auction house, the auctioneer, the merchandise, and each other, they can be helpful and amusing.

Most important, the pre-sale display is where you can take a good look at the merchandise and decide if any of it interests you and, if so, how much. At some establishments, these few minutes before the sale may be your last opportunity to view what is going up before the individual article actually stands on the block. At some galleries—especially the more elegant—nothing is visible during the sale save what is being bid upon. At other places, the merchandise is visible, usually at the front or to one side of the seating area, but the crowd is not encouraged to inspect the merchandise while the sale is in progress. In some houses, inspection is forbidden once the sale begins. There are establishments that do permit viewing during the sale; these, for some reason, tend to be the auctions with the most haphazard approach to display so that viewing consists of crawling about stacks of things in full view of an appreciative audience. Less extroverted auctiongoers may feel uncomfortable at finding themselves part of the show.

This brings up the question of how early to arrive at the auction. One of the delights of auctiongoing is that you can come and go as you choose. If you want to arrive late and leave early, no one will think anything of it as long as you do not disrupt the sale.

Still, to inspect the merchandise and to have time to observe your fellow auctiongoers, you must arrive at the auc-

tion place ahead of the time of the sale. Just how far ahead depends on how much time you think you will need. Generally, the establishment will admit customers as early as an hour before sale time. And that brings us to the reliability of posted sale times. If a house has advertised that a sale will begin at 1:30 P.M., Saturday the 20th, the sale will be on Saturday the 20th, but the sale may start anytime after 1:30. It is rare for a sale to start even a few minutes early, but fairly normal for sales to start ten to fifteen minutes late. Sometimes the late start is due to a tardy auctioneer or to the absent consignor who insisted on being present during the entire sale. Sometimes the sound equipment goes on the blink (the sound equipment at auctions seems always on the brink of the blink). Or maybe it's just that the crowd is still smallish, and the house wants to wait a few minutes to see if a better crowd will gather in the meantime. To be on the safe side, you should plan to arrive at least ten minutes before the advertised starting time if you wish to attend the sale from the beginning.

To return to our mythical auction, let's assume that you've completed your inspection of the merchandise and have found a couple of things that interest you. Now is the time to make sure that these items will be sold at this sale. Do not assume that just because something is sitting in the area where the sale is to be held, it will be auctioned. Some of the merchandise may be part of the house's permanent display furniture; some may represent features of primarily decorative interest that—if they are for sale at all—are to be sold retail and not by auction. If you have a list of what is to be sold, numbered according to order, corresponding to numbers on the furniture, you can tell easily what will come up. Otherwise, find an employee of the auction house (usually a few of the helpers and sometimes the auctioneer will be standing around before the sale begins) and ask him if what you are interested in is due to come up today.

Expressing an interest in an item is especially important at houses where items that have obviously attracted audience interest are the first to go up. At some houses, the ones that have much more merchandise sitting around than they intend to sell at any one time, the sale is mostly composed of requested items. I have been to at least two auction houses where the auctiongoer was expected to indicate the objects of his interest by attaching self-stick symbols to them. Once the sale began, only those items so marked were brought up by the floor man. Do not, however, express too much interest. An auctiongoer obviously determined to have a lot at any price will usually be forced to bid an inflated amount.

If the auction house employee assures you that what you like will be sold at this session, you now need to find a seat. Most auctions do not take advance reservations for seats. If the auction you are attending does accept reservations, then you will notice that some seats are labelled with the names or numbers of auctiongoers. It is not considered good form to pre-empt these seats and may, indeed, lead to embarrassing confrontations. If you have reserved a seat, then find the chair with your name on it. If there are no reserved seats, then you are free to sit wherever you choose—provided that no one else has claimed the chair by putting a coat or notebook or some other personal belonging on it.

There is some dispute as to the best place to sit. Many experienced auctiongoers, especially dealers, are fond of the rear of the hall. From there they can watch the bidding and see who is contending with them. Others would not be caught dead sitting anywhere but toward the front. It is true that from the front you have a much better view of the merchandise as it is put on the block. If you have not looked carefully at all the merchandise before the sale begins, you will probably be happier sitting toward the front.

Once seated you can watch the activity around you. The hall will be a bustle of noise and movement with auctiongoers milling about watching the merchandise and each other. The employees will begin to take their places for the sale. Numbers and exact duties may vary, but you can usually expect to see these basic personnel at almost any auction: a record clerk to register the sale results; a cashier to collect for the merchandise sold; a floor man who directs the during-sale display of merchandise; helpers who actually show the merchandise to the crowd; a clerk to distribute sold merchandise to the auctiongoers who have successfully bid upon and paid for it; and, of course, an auctioneer.

If the sale is to be a long one, there may be more than one auctioneer so that the men may rotate the auctioneering chores. At some houses you will notice a security guard, usually an off-duty policeman hired by the house to discourage any unauthorized and unscheduled activities like robbery.

As sale time approaches, the auctioneer will mount the podium or get behind the desk or whatever else indicates his position and turn on the sound equipment, which almost invariably crackles and hisses. After a quick look at the crowd, he will then bang his gavel and announce that he is beginning the sale. If the terms of sale are not printed on a list to be distributed or are not posted prominently at several points around the hall, the auctioneer will briefly state the conditions under which the house sells. However they may be expressed, at most auctions the terms of sale are basically these: (1) all sales are cash (or credit card); (2) all sales are final; (3) the house assumes no responsibility

for the description or authenticity of the items to be sold, as they are on display for you to see with your own eyes; (4) if there is any dispute over a sale, the auctioneer has the final word; (5) the house has the right to place reserves (either express or implied) on certain items, that is, to set prices below which certain items may not be sold; (6) you are expected to take your purchases with you or at least to pick them up within a specified number of days; (7) if you do not pick up merchandise within the stated time, the house has the right to resell; (8) in any event, the house assumes no responsibility for the condition of any articles left with them for any length of time. Not every auction proceeds under these exact terms, but they are fairly standard so that you may expect most of them to govern almost any sale that you attend.

Listen to these terms carefully; this is important in a legal sense if you later feel that you have been stung. The terms under which most auction houses sell (and their interpretation of them) make your friendly local loan shark look generous in comparison, so it is best to be forewarned. What the auctioneer, his helpers, or any other auction house employee or even the consignors say during the sale about what will or will not be done regarding merchandise or any claims that they make for merchandise is—in a legal sense—usually meaningless if it conflicts with the stated terms of sale. The terms are all that matter. If you do not feel that you will be comfortable playing this game in which the other side has all the odds in its favor, now is the time to decide.

If you stay, you may hear the auctioneer give a brief rundown on the system of bidding to be used at the auction. Most of the auctions that we have been considering use the simple system where bidding is competitive and advances in regular units until the point where no one else will make a bid, at which time the merchandise is knocked down to the last and highest bidder.

There are other sorts of auctions; however, the only variety that you are likely to encounter with any degree of regularity is the Dutch auction, so called because it derives from the method of selling valuable tulip bulbs in the Netherlands. In this country, Dutch auction means that the auctioneer will state a price on an article, then decrease the price in regular units. The first person in the audience to signify acceptance of the price so stated is the successful bidder.

Usually the auctioneer will welcome the audience to the sale, and his remarks will give you an idea of what is to come. The auctioneer who drawls, "We've got some nice things, some mediocre that you can take home and tinker with," is anticipating an entirely different kind of sale from the man who announces gravely, "There is some really fine merchandise to be sold today, and I see a lot of people here who know quality.''

Unless the auctioneer plugs an upcoming sale, this generally ends the preliminaries. If the sale is a very specialized one and the auctioneer considers himself an authority on what is being sold, he may give a brief talk on the highlights of the sale to come and perhaps mention some of the finer points of collecting in this field.

With the prologue out of the way, the sale will then begin. The first piece of merchandise will be placed on the block or held up before the crowd, and the auctioneer will begin hunting for bids. There are about as many different ways of calling bids as there are auctioneers to call them. The tobacco-style auctioneer maintains a continuous drone as he chants the call that makes it difficult to reproduce the effect with any degree of versimilitude. Auctioneers favoring other styles tend to be both slower and less noisy. Below is a common approach:

> No. 1 on your list, an interesting old vase, good color. Who'll give me $10? $10? $5? $5? $2.50 I'm bid; who'll make it $5? $3 I'm bid; who'll make it $4? $4? $4? $4? Will anyone bid $4? Sold to No. 104 for $3.

Here, you notice, the auctioneer sets what he considers a desirable (or at least an optimistic) opening figure. When no one comes in to bid at that point, he halves the figure. Still no one comes in, and the auctioneer accepts a bid of $2.50, which he tries to advance to $5. No one will bid $5, but a second bidder advances the bid to $3. When the auctioneer is unable to get an advance over $3 after a reasonable effort, he sells the vase to auctiongoer No. 104, who made the successful $3 bid.

It is within the auctioneer's power to refuse to start the item on the block for less than a certain amount, if he feels that it is not in the best interest of the house to do so, in which event something like this will occur:

> No. 46 on your list. A beautiful, antique Sheffield candelabrum. Very good condition. Will you bid $200 for this beautiful candelabrum? $200? Then will you bid $150? $150? Will you bid $100? I really don't feel we should start it for less than that. It is truly a lovely old piece of work. Well, will you start it at $75? $75? $75? No one will start for $75? Then we must pass it and move along.

The matter of how much the advance should be is also up to the auctioneer. The audience may offer any advance, but the auctioneer is within his rights in refusing to accept an advance that he finds inappropriate, thus:

> No. 55 on your list. A satinwood drop leaf Pembroke table with crossbanded top. Mint condition. Original hardware. Probably early nineteenth century. Who'll give me $500 for this fine table? $400? $300? Then what will you bid? $100, I have $100. Who'll make it $200? $125, I have $125. Who'll make it $150? $150, I have $150. Who'll make it $175? $175? $175? No sir, I'm sorry I cannot accept an advance of $5. Not at these prices. $150, $150 I have. Who'll make it $175? I will take $160. Do I hear $160? $160, I have $160. Who'll make it $170? $170? $170? I have $170; who'll make it $180? $190? $200? $200, I have $200. Who'll make it $210? $220? $220, I have $220. Who'll make it $230? $230? $230? $230? $230? $230? Sold to No. 79, $220.

This kind of auctioneer is easy to follow once you have absorbed the pattern of his bid calling, which is not difficult provided the auctioneer enunciates reasonably well and the sound system is adequate. It is also possible to understand (eventually) even fast tobacco-style auctioneers, as their pattern is equally locked in, although the specific rendition of it may vary from auctioneer to auctioneer. From a tobacco-style auctioneer, you will hear something like this:

> Who'll give me $5? $4? $3? Half, half, would you go a half? Got $3 now. Half, half, would you go a half? Got $3.50 now. Half, half, would you go a half? Half, half, would you go a half? $4 anywhere? Last call. $3.50, No. 16.

At a Dutch auction, the bid calling will go something like this:

> A very handsome oil of an old gentleman, late 1800s, looks to be. Good frame. Do I hear $100? $100? $95? $95? $90? $90? $85? $85? $80? $80? $75? $75? Nobody needs an ancestor, huh? $70? $70? $65? $65? You don't like this old gentleman? $60? $60? $55? $55? $50? $50? You're not all asleep out there, are you? $50? $50? $45? $45? $40? $40? This has to stop somewhere. $40? $40? $35? $35? $35, I have. No. 4.

If two bidders, say No. 4 and No. 20, have simultaneously accepted the $35 price for the portrait, this will probably happen:

> $35? $35? $35 I have in two places. Will one of you make it $37.50. $37.50 I have. Will you make it $40? No? then it is sold at $37.50 to No. 4.

This brings us to the matter of who is spotting bids. Most auctioneers spot their own bids; some depend almost entirely on floor men to spot for them. Usually both the auctioneer and the chief floor man spot bids, with an assist from the record clerk. At some auctions, several helpers also spot, which can lead to confusion. If there is a dispute, in principle the auctioneer has the final say; his decision may be as arbitrary as he chooses since he is in much the same position as the captain of a ship at sea.

Many auctiongoers think that they have bid successfully on merchandise, then get very upset when it is knocked down to someone else. This is sometimes the fault of the person or people spotting bids. More often, at least in my observation, it is the fault of the auctiongoer. Many auctiongoers simply do not know how to bid successfully. In talking with several auctioneers, I heard the same thing over and over: tell people to bid where we can see them and in a manner that is unmistakable. One floor man even expressed a preference for loud voice bids in the form of "$5, here!" or "I will" in response to the auctioneer's spiel. Most auctioneers feel that a raised hand or a waved registration number is adequate for the initial bid on an item. Once the initial bid is made, the auctioneer's eye will be on you until the item is sold, so after the initial bid you may be less obvious if you choose. Usually all that is required is a brisk nod when the auctioneer looks your way to see if you are willing to advance someone else's bid.

There is a school of thought that holds that procrastination is a businesslike tactic and likely to produce lower final prices. Whether this is true or not is difficult to prove. Quick bidding, however, has several obvious advantages. Decisiveness always impresses an auctioneer, and he will notice you much more carefully if you bid in a manner that plainly shows that you know your own mind. Hesitate, and he may be looking at someone else and taking their bid for the same amount that you had in mind. Hesitate still more, and the item may be knocked down just as you begin to nod your acceptance. It is impossible to bid decisively unless you have made a decision about the merchandise, but we will go into that later.

The old days when people used to bid by winking the right eyelid or wiggling the left foot or lighting a cigarette at the crucial moment live no more save at certain high fashion sales where some dealers and old-time collectors enjoy playing this little game. A few people at the average auction may have discussed bidding signals with the auctioneer ahead of time, but their number is miniscule. Gauche as waving one's hand about may seem, it beats remembering when to yawn and, more importantly, when not to.

Whatever approach to bidding an individual auctiongoer may prefer, it is essential that he be able to tell when bidding is about to be closed on an item. Different auctioneers use different signals. The more obliging will announce, "Last call," when they have milked an item as long as they intend to. Others may change their voice pitch or the rhythm of the call. I know one auctioneer who always lifts his left eyebrow just before closing the bid. To tell how a particular auctioneer handles the approaching bid closing, watch him carefully as several items sell, and usually a pattern will emerge. If you see that the bid is about to be closed and are uncertain if the bid is yours, ask the auctioneer or floor man. You may get some irritated looks, but at least you'll know and won't risk bidding against yourself or losing something that you thought was already yours.

When you bid successfully on an item, the auctioneer will signify that this lot is sold, then will turn to you for your identification. If you have been given a registration card or paddle with your number on it, now is the time to hold it,

right side up, facing the auctioneer. If you were not given this form of identification, call out your number or your name, if you have no number. After you have identified yourself, the auctioneer will intone to his record clerk: "Item No. 78, $37.50 to No. 14."

If the successful bid is disputed at this point, the auctioneer will ordinarily reopen the bidding; so if you have a protest, now is the time to voice it. Otherwise, you may have lost something needlessly or may wind up paying more than you thought you bid.

When your bid is successful, one of two things will happen. At some country sales, you may be asked to pay the amount that you bid as soon as the sale of the item is completed. At most sales, however, the house keeps a running record of your purchases. As they say, "Go and do ye likewise." Houses have been known to err. When a running record is kept, you may settle for all your purchases at the end of the sale or whenever you leave the premises. (If you find it necessary to leave during the sale, but plan to return before its completion, you should keep your auction number and inform the cashier that you will be back. Otherwise, the house may think that you are trying to sneak out without paying for what you have bought. Some houses will insist that you settle up before leaving, even if you consider your departure only temporary.)

When you are ready to leave the auction, go to the cashier and state your name or number. The cashier will get from the record clerk the invoice bearing your identification. On the invoice, all the merchandise on which you bid successfully will be listed. The cashier will total these figures, add any applicable local taxes, then ask you for that exact amount. Most houses will allow you to pay by either check or cash. Some auction houses honor BankAmericard, Master Charge, and regional credit cards. Others will establish monthly accounts for regular customers, but this procedure must be worked out in advance of the sale.

At most auctions, what you've bought is not delivered to your seat on completion of bidding unless it is small. Anything else is put in the house's sold room or in a section where sold merchandise is stored. If what you have bought is small enough for you to carry out (and you'd be surprised how much you can cram in even a VW, given the proper incentive), then you present your invoice marked "paid" by the cashier to the clerk responsible for distribution of sold merchandise. He or she will get it for you and check your invoice to the effect that you have picked up the merchandise. If what you have bought is too large for such casual treatment, you may be forced to leave it at the auction house and return for it later. If this is the case, have the cashier note on the invoice that you will return for the merchandise.

Never leave merchandise at an auction house any longer than absolutely necessary. Most auction houses reserve for themselves the right to resell any merchandise left on their premises beyond a specified number of days unless special arrangements have been made. And you may not get your money back should this happen. Also, there is the danger that your merchandise may be deliberately or accidentally picked up by someone else. Since the house usually assumes no responsibility for any merchandise left with them, you are simply out the money should this happen. Some houses, even those claiming otherwise, will make good, but don't count on it.

If you buy something too big to take home on the day of the auction, make sure to have your "paid" invoice with you when you return to pick it up. Memorable though you may be, the staff members of a busy establishment see a lot of faces and even more merchandise in the course of a sale; you should have that invoice to establish your claim beyond all doubt. When you present the invoice to the auction house employee, he will note the number on it (the registration number from the sale) and find the item marked with the corresponding number or symbol. Once found, the item will be given to you and the fact noted on the invoice. The boys at the house may help you to get it in your car or truck in the expectation of a small tip.

By now you may be wondering why you should have to bother with picking up what you bought. Why shouldn't the house bring it to you? Auction house operators reach a rare unanimity in agreeing that delivery is a pain that they are extremely reluctant to develop. Therefore, many of them give no delivery assistance at all, including both local delivery and packing for shipment elsewhere. Those who do offer such assistance generally charge handsomely for their efforts. Thus, be prepared to hoist upon your own back anything that you buy at auction. (Now you know why those grand pianos always go so cheap.)

Most of the time you will have no difficulty in claiming merchandise within the house's grace period. If, however, you return within that period and find your merchandise missing, now is the time to kick up a fuss. It may be that the house will make no adjustment anyway; but your chances of getting one now are better than they will be next week or next month after the staff "checks" and procrastinates.

If you feel aggrieved that the burden of removal lies too heavily on you and think that the least that the house can do is to provide storage until it is convenient for you to pick up that giant wardrobe or turn-of-the-century steamer trunk, I couldn't agree with you more. Maybe we should form a lobby because that's probably the only way the houses will agree to deliver. The operators protest that they're in business to move merchandise, not store or deliver it.

There will be variations in procedure at almost every auction you attend. That is why it is so important that you carefully watch what goes on before attempting to bid. Understanding a house's setup can make you a more satsified auctiongoer, and this goal is worth the effort to attain it.

Paying close attention at auction is both important and difficult because of all the distractions.

Auctions are rarely quiet. People talk, laugh, walk around. The auctioneer cuts up. The auction staff pulls little gags, visual and otherwise, to liven things up. Parents sometimes loose young children to crawl about the hall, choosing at random which ankles to molest and when to emit ear-piercing screams. Occasionally flashbulbs go off as someone photographs the sale. Drunks bait the auctioneer. Determined competitors have been known to approach fisticuffs over a debated lot. My own favorite auction house was robbed not long ago.

Things happen at auctions. There was the sale in Boston a few years ago when three Shirley Temple dolls were put up for the sale and the auctioneer impulsively broke into "On the Good Ship Lollipop"; the catchy refrain was speedily picked up by the whole house. Jazz pianists have been known to leap from their seats to give an impromptu performance on a piano or organ going up. Floor men have been seen to strap on accordions and prance about, yodeling "Lady of Spain." Helpers pull the old drawer-out-of-control routine, making the front row jump from their seats.

Since one of the prime attributes of a good auctioneer is his ability to loosen up a nervous audience or to keep an affable audience in a good mood, every auction provides laughs. Some of them are directed at the auctiongoers themselves.

> I wasn't sure if you were bidding or just raising your glass in a toast.
>
> Come on, don't listen to him. He's only your husband. Listen to *me*.
>
> I know you've got all the money in the world, Joe; why don't you spend some of it—like now?
>
> The hot dogs and hamburgers are here for those of you who came thinking this was a restaurant.

And the merchandise itself comes in for a share of the yuks:

Of a Mason's ironstone potty: That's a mighty big coffee cup.

Of a worn, mediocre oriental rug, going very low: Is this an oriental or a grass rug?

Of a heavy silver bowl: A Tiffany bowl, by sterling.

Of a mismatched sterling salad set: They're probably so old that they didn't know how to make them exactly alike back then.

Of a box full of assorted old-time medicine bottles and other drug store paraphenalia: Creomulsion—Dr. Sloan's—and, ooh-oh, some of *those*!

Of a set of sixteen Napoleonic porcelain Marshalls: All those guys, and he still couldn't beat 'em.

Of a large brass coal bucket shaped like a helmet: Sell it. It's enough for it. You folks are mighty big on buckets.

The auctioneer will even get a laugh out of the fact that he is "hurting" at the low prices:

Are you folks sure you came to an auction?

You're seeing history made here this evening. Others make highs. We're making lows.

Funny, this doesn't *look* like a crowd needing charity.

I know most of you people haven't seen prices like this in a long time; I hope I never see them again!

Each of the above quotes brought at least titters of amusement at one sale or another, and a couple proved to be absolute sideholders. Weak as auction room humor is, the audience almost always laughs, albeit shakily at times. Why? Because most of them are there to buy something, to spend money. This usually has one of two effects on most people. It makes them so nervous that they would laugh at the Gettysburg Address recited in an Italian dialect by a Greek auctioneer; or it relaxes them so that they are in a generous mood, prepared to cooperate with the auctioneer's efforts and to find the mildest jest quite funny. The humor in the auction is but another manifestation of the strange mixture of greed and desire, frustration and wish fulfillment.

For the space of time that you are in an auction, you are in another world where the language is a little different, the merchandise often on the unusual side, the people you meet sometimes more than a little eccentric. In this world, anything can happen, as long as the crazy consistency of the auction is maintained. Here the word China conjures up thoughts not of politics and politicians, but of old silk hangings and delicate porcelain. A rise in the market is more likely to refer to the slow but steady recovery of old carnival glass than to ticker tape tabulations.

It is often a tawdry world, always bittersweet, but it is fascinating. Besides, where else can you furnish your house while sitting comfortably, sipping something cold and wet, while a lot of energetic people outdo themselves trying to amuse and please you?

Chapter 8

Auction Trends

Like everything else on spaceship earth, auctions do not remain static. Their basic form may remain generally the same, but different parts of the form may vary considerably from year to year and sometimes, it seems, from sale to sale. There may be a change in the numbers and kind of people attending, the merchandise on the block, and the prices offered. The trend is not smooth, but in a state of continual flux. Several auctioneers and long-time auctiongoers put forth some interesting, if not always compatible, ideas about current trends.

There seems to be a consensus of opinion that the average age of auction audiences grows steadily younger. All over the country, young people are gradually discovering the auction, just as they have taken to their hearts the dusty junque shops, flea markets, and Goodwill stores. They have learned that the auction is an excellent source for the off-beat, the out-of-the-ordinary, the cheap but usable item. Many of the old hands do not like this development and are not above snickering at floor-length purple ponchos trimmed in orange fringe or at handsomely groomed young men with hair that Breck might covet. But the youth wave is definitely here.

There also seems to be general agreement that almost all auctiongoers, but especially these younger newcomers, are willing to spend more easily than were their predecessors in the auction hall; and a lot of this spending is being done with credit cards. The old days of cash before you carry are long gone. Credit is much looser; people are making more, anticipate making still more in the future, and are willing to spend in advance of their actual receipt of this income. This is a well known phenomenon, and we need only note that it has affected the auction as well as all other areas of American life.

Perhaps as a by-product of this fiscal confidence, auctioneers note that audiences today bid in a more straightforward manner with less of the old coyness. "Most people today know pretty well what they want and how much they're willing to pay for it," one man told me, "and all of your coaxing won't budge them by much."

"People today are definitely more sophisticated about their buying," another auctioneer agreed. "I think that this is reflected most in the fact that we get fewer post-sale complaints about misunderstandings now than we did even ten years ago."

The number of people coming to auctions is much greater today than it was a few years ago, according to most observers. One reason put forth for this development is that people who only a short time ago would not have had anything old or used in their homes have discovered the charms of the antique and the eclectic, both as a pleasant adjunct to modern life and as proof that they are *au courant*.

Apart from dealers, most auctiongoers of yesteryear tended to be either people who had grown up with the sale, who had been dandled from Daddy's knee while a country auctioneer pleaded for "a half, a half, gimme a half," or else people who were primarily interested in higher quality sales but became regulars at garden variety auctions as well. Today almost anybody can turn up at auction and usually does. There is no reason to suppose that this trend will reverse. Rather, it is possible that we will see an intensification of the trend as new auctiongoers, delighted with their discovery, tell friends, who come and tell still other friends. Another reason suggested for the continually in-

creasing crowds is the high price and often inferior quality of so much new merchandise. Too, the contemporary desire for individuality, increasingly reflected in the home and its decoration, demands merchandise not available by the gross in your local shopping center. The auction certainly offers variety and often uniqueness. (I mean, not many of your friends will have a souvenir clock from the 1939 World's Fair, now will they?) It also offers a range of merchandise comparable with that offered by any but the most sophisticated department stores.

Perhaps it is due to the growing popularity of the auction, but one auctioneer declared that there is much more flux in audiences today. "At one time, I could call 60 percent of the people in any of my auctions by their first name; I knew them that well. Today, if I know 20 percent of them by their last names, I feel that it's old home week."

I asked him about the dealers; did they still form the core of the average auction?

> Yes, to some extent, but the dealers—at least in my house—don't give the same sort of support that they once did. It used to be that dealers snapped up almost any sort of item going for a good price, even if they hadn't thought about buying it before the sale. This was good for us because it gave us a block of support bidders who kept any nice merchandise from going too low. It was good for them because it gave them a wide variety of stock. And if they couldn't use everything they bought themselves, they could usually sell it or consign it to another dealer who didn't get to auctions enough. Today it's a whole different story. Dealers are often not content with a reasonable markup. That's one reason why you see such high prices in the antique shops. That's also one reason why most shops have such a slow turnover. They won't support bid any more because they have to get things so cheap to make this big markup.

Some of the markup, he admitted, is due to much increased overhead in the form of shop rents, salaries, and other continuing office expenses.

Mostly, however, especially when you're talking about the higher quality merchandise, it's the interior decorators. It's natural that a decorator be paid a finder's commission by his client, in one form or another. A lot of decorators, however, don't limit themselves to that. Say decorator Jones, redoing Mrs. Prince's house, sees a sideboard in the window of Jervis' shop that he feels will be ideal for the Prince dining room. He will call on Jervis, inform him that he is planning on bringing Mrs. Prince in that afternoon to look at the sideboard and that, if she buys it, he expects to be paid a percentage of the selling price. Of course, Jones is being paid by Mrs. Prince also. Jervis knows this, and Jones knows that he knows. That makes no difference. If Jervis wants to sell that sideboard—which is an expensive piece and may be hard to move otherwise—he has to go along. So the price marked on the sideboard reflects not only Jervis' normal markup, but also Jones' extra cut. Because this practice violates the stated ethics of their professional organizations, really reputable decorators won't do it; but enough disreputable ones exist to make it a fairly common practice.

And what of prices at tomorrow's auctions? Almost everyone concerned is convinced that they will continue to rise. "They can't help but rise. There's just so much old stuff, and there are a lot more people wanting it all the time," one man said. "They're buying as a hedge against inflation."

Auction prices tomorrow may reflect an interesting development: the increasing dependence of many auction houses on imports, both old and new. As imports become more important, the houses will own outright more and more of what they are auctioning. It could well be that this will lead to an increased desire on the part of the houses to "protect" prices.

All this brings us to the trend in merchandise. Just what kind of goods will appear on the block in the future? There is, obviously, a limit to the supply of old things. Will this fact mean a decrease in goods for auction? "Not at all," said one auctioneer:

> It may be a different sort of merchandise, but more not less will go on the block. People are learning that dealers are just too cautious about buying large, diversified blocks of merchandise where at auction almost anything can be sold at a reasonable price. Auction offers the average consignor a much better chance of getting a fair, current market price for his merchandise than any other method of disposal, even after we deduct our commission from the selling price. Too, you must remember that as time goes by, everything gets older, including furniture and collectibles. Something that looks like nothing on the block today may seem a very desirable part of a sale in a few years. Furniture that was used twenty years ago is described as old today, and twenty years from now—the way things are going—will be called antique.

Up until a few years ago, to be an "antique" in America, an item had to have been made prior to 1830. In 1966, this definition was updated by federal law so that goods become antique on a sliding scale: anything made one hundred years or more from today is officially an antique. Thus, much as it may devastate the Chippendale fanatics, much of the Victorian furniture in the style of Eastlake is on the verge of becoming antique if it has not already reached that lofty state. Everything in the Empire and Early Victorian periods has been antique for long enough to have become quite respectable in even the most refined circles. Just ask Amy Vanderbilt if you don't believe me; her townhouse in New York is a veritable museum of furniture from this era as well as earlier times.

Purists insist that the term "antique" carries a quality implication as well as an age designation. To them, an antique must be the work of hand craftsmen, designing and creating in the traditions that were mostly abandoned when almost all furniture and pottery crafts went increasingly to machinery during the nineteenth century. Using this approach, an 1840 chest made in a primitive German factory is merely old, a 1900 vase of art nouveau persuasion from the workshop of an English craftsman is antique.

The word "antique" is bandied about freely in the world of the auction, particularly in advertising sales. Most auctioneers call "antique" anything that has lost its original shine. In auction house terminology, "antique" is a word meant to call forth pleasant associative images from the customer, images that will make him place a higher value on the object than he would otherwise. It is simply a catch-all phrase to describe anything that may look even remotely old or be in the style, however distant, of something old.

In private, auction house operators and auctioneers tend to be more frank about their wares. "We never planned to handle anything but old American items, real antiques," confessed one operator, "but that proved to be almost impossible. We're not selling antiques today. We're selling used furniture. If we get an antique on that block it's unusual."

"Just a few years ago," another operator moaned, "we were selling things at auction that were of such quality any shop in this city would snap them up today, and we were selling them cheap. Now most of our so-called antiques are second-rate Empire and fair-to-good quality Victorian, and we're seeing more and more of the turn-of-the-century Grand Rapids furniture. The situation has changed radically."

The traditional wholesale sources of supply, according to many operators, are beginning to dry up. Country auction houses relying on haulers have become especially conscious of this. "They say it's harder and harder to get good things," said one operator. "Taste is becoming more uniform throughout the U.S., and the same kind of merchandise is becoming popular almost everywhere, which means that the haulers have to pay such high prices that it's unlikely they'll make a profit after their expenses."

Voicing a similar lament was the operator of an auction gallery that depends to some extent on imports. "Europe is almost picked dry of good, old merchandise," claimed this man. "From now on you're going to see a lot of very good European reproductions."

According to the auction pros, it looks as if we're going to see—along with a flood of imports, old and new—a lot of interwar bric-a-brac, much more Victorian furniture of better than average quality, a steady stream of post-1900, even post-1920 furniture of better than average quality, and inevitably, many new reproductions of old styles in all kinds of merchandise.

This is not meant to imply that older, even antique merchandise will not continue to appear, especially if prices continue to rise as they have in recent years. As the proprietor of one country auction told me, "If I sell a golden oak table for $400, golden oak starts coming out of the walls, the same for any other article that begins to bring exceptional prices. People who bought when prices were lower pretty often decide they'd rather consign the article to auction to get that kind of price than hang onto it."

Reproductions have posed a particular problem for the auction house. Certain American glass companies that own molds for glassware first produced a century and more ago are cashing in on the desire for this glassware by reinstating production. Carnival glass and milk glass have been reproduced so beautifully that the new is sometimes superior in quality to the old, according to some glass devotees. Before these excellent reproductions, both carnival and milk glass were hot items at both auction and shop. Afterwards, their auction prices tended to decline dramatically. Many people felt, and quite reasonably, that it was pointless to buy, at collector's prices, glass that might or might not be old, when one could call up a department store and order the new, admittedly lovely variety at a much lower cost. Now, however, the impact of these reproductions has been absorbed, and prices are again on the increase for old carnival and milk glass. One auctioneer predicted that this pattern would endure, that good reproductions of any item would initially drive down its value, but that the effect would be only temporary—at which time the main danger of reproductions to the collector was that they might fool even him into accepting them as originals.

If the people, the prices, and the merchandise are in a state of constant flux in the auction world, what about the auction itself: will it continue in its present form? In the most basic sense, probably yes. There still must be goods,

someone to sell them, someone to buy them, and some place where they are to be sold. Any changes will probably come in the periphery of auctions. As auction houses proliferate and competition becomes more intense, they may find it to their advantage to offer somewhat more in the way of service. Many of the auctiongoers whom they may wish to attract will have been reared in the Macy's syndrome and will think it somewhat cumbersome, for example, that they are expected to trundle away eight-foot sideboards in their Fiats.

It is my guess that many of the better capitalized houses will make some effort at increasing the amenities at their auctions. Already there seems to be a trend toward the provision of better seating and the availability of refreshments of varying kinds. I think that more sophisticated advertising techniques will be employed by the houses and that display techniques, especially in the big-city auctions, will become more elaborate. In just the few years that I have been attending sales, I have noticed a definite trend away from the "let's just stack it any old way" school and toward the more artful arrangements pioneered by the department stores. Larger auction houses will employ more of the machine-oriented technology developed by big business so that more merchandise can be moved and more customers served without any significant increase in the number of personnel.

In other words, I think that the physical appearance and, to some extent, operation of tomorrow's auction houses will reflect the fact that auctions today are attracting more of the general public than ever before and that these people will not find many of the old practices acceptable. Auctions have already ceased to be the sole property of the steady few; their progress into the realm of the many will require some readjustments.

It seems that the auction business is at the point of an important decision. It can jealously guard its old ways and the customers used to them, or it can adapt itself to the quite different expectations of its larger potential clientele. Until now most auctions have maintained a refreshingly independent air implying that the customer was welcome to stay but that the house had no intention of neglecting its important business—the movement of goods—to bother unduly with him. If the houses opt for adaptability, this may change to the point that the auction becomes much more customer oriented. In some ways, this would be good; but I cannot help wondering if the friendly casualness of the average sale will succumb to self-conscious presentation. Just how much of the dust and the color will the houses be willing to exchange for respectability?

Chapter 9

Common Mistakes and How to Avoid Them

The auction offers enormous potential to the person looking for good buys in terms of price, quality, or uniqueness; yet a surprising number of people who go to auctions come away more dissatisfied than otherwise. They blame the auction house (it's crooked), the auctioneer (he confuses me), the merchandise (everything I buy is no good), the dealers (they bid up the best things so I can't afford them), the non-dealers (the faddists run up prices on everything), and so on. Very little about auctions is to their liking, and they blame everything but the weather for their seeming bad luck. I take that back; some of them do blame the weather (if it weren't such a nice day, there wouldn't be so many people here and prices would be lower). They rarely, if ever, look in the mirror and see the major culprit—themselves.

They expect to go to auction with as little forethought as a leaf falling from a tree; they expect to enjoy themselves; and they expect to come away laden with treasures bought at bargain prices. This is a pretty picture; but like most fairy tales, it is strictly out of Mother Gooseland. When this pleasant sequence of events fails to materialize, our heedless auctiongoer becomes indignant, sputtering that "they" have done him in again.

At this point, I hope that you are not waiting for me (or anyone else) to give you a foolproof formula for gauging the auction house, the auctioneer, the merchandise, and the crowd with one quick glance. I could repeat to you a lot of the things that I have been told, such as, "A smiling auctioneer means the price is too high." And there's always the one about the house that has a lot of employees having to "run up the prices to get all those people paid." Not to mention the fact that everyone *knows* that the best buys come from the shabby houses with the "just plain folks" auctioneers.

When I first began going to auctions, this kind of talk bothered me. Now it makes me mad because it obscures what is to me the whole point of the sale: to obtain merchandise that I like at a price I can afford and am willing to pay. To me the people who look to see how well the staff is dressed are playing the auction game. There is nothing wrong with this game; but—being part Scot—I find it hard to risk money on a game. And if I didn't have this ancestral disability, I would go to Las Vegas or Monte Carlo where they really know how to gamble and don't delude themselves that they are doing anything else.

Understand, I'm not knocking the game for other people; and if you enjoy playing it and won't be upset when black instead of red turns up, you can save yourself some time by skipping this chapter and the next. You are one of those happy people (and at times I envy you) who can take the auction as it comes. Since pleasure and not acquisition is your aim, you don't need to do anything to achieve your goal but attend the sale.

To those of you who are still with me, never forget that your best, indeed your only, ally in the auction hall is your own common sense. If you observe what goes on around you and learn from your own conclusions, you will be a much more contented auctiongoer than if you listen to all the old "truths." For one thing, many of them are not al-

ways true; for another, you can do little about some of them that are, no matter how much certain practices outrage your idea of what is fair.

There are undoubtedly crooked houses, confusing auctioneers, lousy merchandise, canny dealers, and mad spenders in the auction world; but wishing will not make them vanish. The secret is to relegate them to a proper perspective. Look at the process sensibly. There is nothing that you can do about canny dealers and mad spenders, so you might as well not let them upset you. As for the auction house and the auctioneer, they are no more than intermediaries between you and the merchandise. They cannot use you unless you are subconsciously willing. They cannot manipulate you unless you are vulnerable. What makes you vulnerable is the fact that you are unsure of what you are doing and why. When you gain confidence through knowledge, you will be in a position to use the auction to further your own ends; the people who stage it will no longer be able to prey upon your uncertainty.

The purpose of this chapter is to point out some of the most common mistakes auctiongoers make and how they may be avoided. As the basis for our discussion, we have the opinions and comments of both long-time auctioneers (who were surprisingly willing to point out where auctiongoers go wrong) and experienced auctiongoers.

According to our experts, most auctiongoers who leave the sale unhappy do so because:

1. They don't know how to read auction ads, so they come expecting an entirely different kind of auction from the one scheduled.
2. They don't understand the terms of sale.
3. They are easily confused by rumors and the comments of the people around them.
4. They don't follow the bidding carefully enough.
5. They don't know merchandise.
6. They don't know values.
7. They complain about dishonest auction houses, yet continue to patronize them.

How do you read an auction ad? Carefully, say the pros. Just as in all other forms of advertising, the businessman (in this instance, the auction house proprietor) will present his product (the auction) as appealingly as possible. Keep in mind that many auction operators are prone to poetic license when describing the contents of their next sale and that others grudge an extra word to publicize a bargain sale of Picassos. Still, there are certain things to look or to listen for in auction advertising that will give you a fairly accurate idea of what kind of sale is being puffed.

First, there are certain tipoff words. "The Sale of a Lifetime" featuring "Fine Investment Pieces" carefully assembled "For Discriminating Collectors" who will find this "A Night to Remember" from the time the "Champagne is Served" until they walk away with their "Treasured Acquisitions" will not consist of stuff from the 1927 Sears & Roebuck catalog (unless the operator has an abnormal amount of nerve). Rather, advertising of this kind almost always indicates an auction of merchandise that is at least meant to be of superior quality, a sale where prices may be as high flown as the ad itself. The average auction will advertise in a less rarefied vein: "Many fine pieces . . . good merchandise . . . low prices." Auction advertising that talks a lot about "friendly folks" and "a real good time" and mentions having "lots of stuff" will usually run more to newer merchandise and less valuable older things.

You can get an idea of the specific items to be auctioned from the brief listing that usually is part of the advertising. High or top quality auctions will advertise eighteenth-century Chinese silk rugs, rosewood grand pianos, French armoires, gilt chandeliers, and coin silver. Auctions in the average range will concentrate on Victorian marble top tables, walnut dressers, round oak tables, china cabinets, Empire sofas, and Victorian plated tea sets. Auctions of the garden variety will advertise that they have wooden refrigerators, washstands, overstuffed couches, phonograph records, and old advertising signs.

Reading auction ads is much simplified when the sale is for a certain kind of collectible, say glass or old advertising matter or dolls. If you are not interested in the collectible, then the sale does not interest you. If you are, then you are competent to interpret the listing.

Not all auction ads are written. Some auction houses, and not just those specializing in higher priced merchandise, have taken to the air waves so that you will occasionally hear ads for auctions on the radio or even see them on television. Here, it is the presentation that will give you an

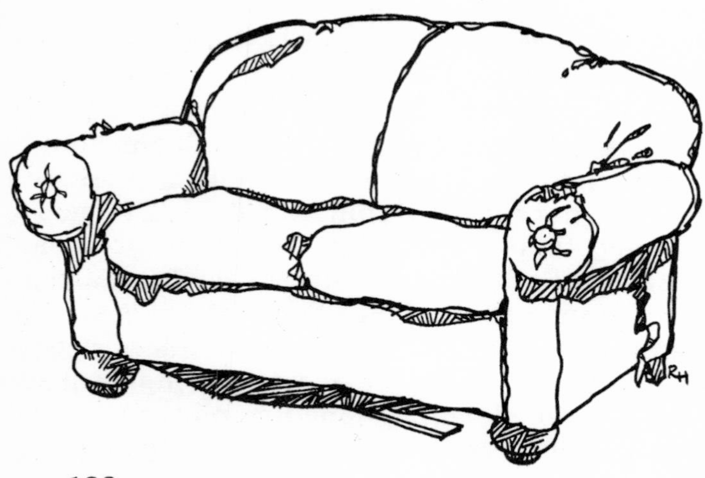

idea of what to expect. If a man with a faked English accent and all the vivacity of an undertaker informs you that Smith Galleries will auction an unusually fine group of collector's furniture and *objets d'art* on Tuesday next (and all the while a Tschaikovsky overture is booming softly in the background), you know that the merchandise will be glittery and the audience well heeled. If the ad turns up on a FM radio station that features nothing but classical music and newscasts dealing mostly with community cultural affairs, you are doubly sure that you will need a fat checkbook or a good line of credit if you intend to do much buying at Smith's.

If, on the other hand, the top forty tunes are interrupted by a breezy voice saying energetically (while *Turkey in the Straw* bounces along just a decibel below voice level): "Come on down. Jo Jo's doin' it again. An auction every Friday night, rain or shine. A lot of friendly folks and good bargains to boot. Plenty of free parking," then the auction is likely to feature a price range that will not intimidate anyone gainfully employed.

One thing to look out for in auction ads is the line, "Contents of the estate of Mrs. F. Throckmorton Browne." As I said before, do not go to that auction expecting all the merchandise to be from Mrs. Browne's own domicile. It is very rare that any sale is composed entirely of goods from one estate; but in areas where the law does not forbid it, some auction houses are not above advertising a sale as being the "estate of . . . " to capitalize on the snob appeal the name may have.

Another thing to watch for is the advertisement that boasts of having been chosen to act as local agents for European consignments. Unless the house doing the advertising is obviously prestigious, such an ad means one of two things: (1) the merchandise is not first rate, even though the house may claim that it is, because first rate European consignments stay in Europe or are sold through the important American auction houses; or (2) the "consignments" are actually the purchases made by the auction house proprietor on his last buying trip to Europe or wherever, in which event their quality may or may not be high, but the prices will almost have to be to cover the house's on-the-line investment in the merchandise.

Interpreting auction advertising properly may seem a minor thing. Still, no matter how well or how badly the house advertises, you should be able to get some idea of what kind of house and what kind of sale to expect. Thus, you do not go prepared to look for old cut glass only to find a plethora of iron wash pots. Remember, most sales are fairly consistent within themselves—they have to be if the house is to make a consistent profit; and most auction operators are clever enough to use advertising to attract the kind of audience that they think will want what they are selling.

Since we've gone into the terms of the sale to some extent in previous chapters, we need only reiterate the importance of understanding them. What the auctioneer or any of the rest of the auction house staff may say during the course of the sale—be it about merchandise or policy—has little legal meaning if it conflicts with the terms of sale. Read the terms of each house carefully if they are printed, or listen closely if they are explained at the start of the sale. If you come in after the auction has begun and cannot find the terms posted anywhere, ask the auctioneer if you have a specific question regarding them. If the house does not offer to reveal its terms before the sale begins, insist that they be spelled out.

The single biggest gripe of many auctiongoers is that some houses will imply a guarantee that doesn't exist. Whether we like it or not, this practice is covered by the terms of most houses. The auctioneer is not—by these terms— responsible for anything that he may say about the merchandise; you buy it as you see it and as you judge it to be. Anything else is just eye wash.

This is as good a place as any to warn you of what seem like guarantees, but do not operate as such in practice. Not long ago I attended a very showy auction, at the beginning of which I was surprised to hear the auctioneer announce that it was the policy of this house to guarantee everything sold as represented. That is, if the auctioneer said that a table was an eighteenth-century table in the Adam style and the purchaser could ultimately prove that it was not, the house would refund his money—and there was no time limit on the guarantee provided the purchaser had kept proof of purchase.

I subsequently mentioned this broad guarantee to another auctioneer, and asked him why this particular house felt it could afford this when most auction houses do not. "Oh yes, their guarantee," he laughed:

> Well, they're very clever about that. I can cite you an example. One of my own customers is suing them right now. Two years ago he was attending one of their sales. They put up a really nice piece of eighteenth-century English furniture, a game table I think, and went into great detail about its aesthetic merits and who had made it and that it had come from the estate of Lord_____, who had an elegant Adam mansion. Then they put up a pair of sideboards which came, they said, from the same mansion. They were, according to the auctioneer, Lord_____'s favorite pieces of furniture in his entire Adam mansion. He had his stuff insured for fifty thousand pounds, they said, and Lord_____ wouldn't have taken anything for these sideboards. Now who would give the auctioneer a start of $10,000 for these unusual and beautiful sideboards? Finally, my customer got them for $7,500 the pair. He later called me in to appraise them, and I saw at once that they certainly weren't what he believed them to be. They were fine furniture, worth maybe $500 each. They were good reproductions, but they were definitely reproductions—1920's, well, let's be charitable, maybe 1900s to stretch it. What the house had done was to put up that antique game table before these sideboards and another genuine antique afterwards. Nowhere did the auctioneer say that these sideboards were antique, just that they came from the same Adam mansion and that they had been old Lord_____'s favorites. That, of course, means nothing. Still, the implication—especially during the excitement of the sale—was that the sideboards were of the same age and

quality as the merchandise preceding and succeeding them. It was a reasonable assumption, but the customer cannot assume in this business.

Another trick of this house and several others that I visited while doing research for this book was that of solemnly assuring a hesitant bidder, "If you don't like this later, you don't have to keep it." They don't, you notice, say that *they* will take it back, only that you don't have to keep it. What this means is that you can give it to Goodwill, put it in the attic, or throw it in the dump; but it sounds like a promise to let you bring the merchandise back if you don't like it later.

View any guarantee with a jaundiced eye and a suspicious mind. Take it in its worst possible meaning, not its best.

Unsophisticated auctiongoers are very susceptible to rumormongers, those creatures who go about before the sale and warn newcomers who are looking at something that they themselves want to buy that "The house is crooked; the auctioneer runs up prices, so you can't get good buys here." This has the effect of making less experienced auctiongoers extremely wary of bidding, and also of eliminating potential competition for the old hands who thus get desirable merchandise much more cheaply than they otherwise would. The new auctiongoers come away frustrated at not buying anything and angry not only at this house, but at the whole auction process.

"Whispering campaigns like this can cost me a lot of money," fumed one auction operator. "And they stem from the desire of regulars to scare away newcomers. These gossips think that if they can keep attendance low, they'll get better buys, which they do. This hurts me, and it hurts the consignors, and it hurts the other auctiongoers. Nobody benefits but the people spreading the stories."

Not all advice that you get at auctions is so obviously self-interested. There is the well meaning woman who taps you on the arm and tells you that the chest on which you're bidding is oak, not cherry as the auctioneer has said, and that furthermore, the price is too high. If you don't know what you're doing and haven't looked at the chest ahead of time, maybe you should listen to the helpful neighbor. It may well be, however, that she only thinks she knows what's what.

Listen noncommittally to the gossips and keep in mind that they may have some purely personal gripe against the house or the auctioneer. It does not hurt to hear gossip, but it is foolish to let it interfere with your own reasoned buying judgments. As for those who would advise you in the midst of the bidding, ignore them if you are sure of the object that interests you. How do you know that they know any more about what is up than you do? They may know a great deal less. (I don't think that there is any field other than antiques that boasts so many experts whose knowledge is superficial at best. You would be surprised, and possibly indignant, at the number of the people in the *trade* who know almost nothing beyond a few well known and overused catch words.) The person so free with advice may see that her cousin Jenny is trying to buy the same thing across the room. She may be a compulsive buttinsky simply trying to impress you. Your best bet is to smile weakly and never take your eyes off the auctioneer. Once you let someone like this engage you in conversation, you have probably lost the bid.

Following the bidding is not always the easiest thing in the world to do anyway, even if you are an old hand. If you are a novice, it can seem almost impossible, but—believe me—it is not, no matter how jumbled it may sound at first. Close attention is the key.

Basically there are three ways for the auctiongoer to bid: in person, in absentia, and by agent. If you have some reason for wanting to conceal your identity, then you will be happier having a knowledgeable friend or trusted dealer bid for you. At big sales in the world-famous auction houses, the major bidding is done mostly by dealers, acting either as agent for collectors or on their own accounts. A dealer will charge you a small percentage of the selling price of the item as a commission, but he may also be able to give you some good advice as to the object's value so that you do not end up paying a sum in excess of that amount. (I am assuming that most of you are not of the "I don't care how much it costs if I like it" school.)

If you do not wish to use an intermediary, but you are not able or do not choose to attend the sale, you may usually leave a bid with the auctioneer, which should be for the amount to which you are willing to go on any particular item or items. Leaving bids has certain advantages and disadvantages. It can save you money under certain conditions, as indicated by the remark of an auction operator who sometimes buys at auction himself to resell: "If you go regularly and consistently buy a certain kind of thing and suspect they're running up prices on you, leave bids for your limit. You'll be surprised at how often items are knocked down to you at your price. Otherwise, you'd have to go more or risk losing the item if you were present during the sale." The main disadvantage of leaving bids is that the auctioneer may not be above running the price up to your bid. That is, you might have gotten the items cheaper if you had been there to bid in person.

One secondary benefit offered by both leaving bids and having an agent bid for you is that it eliminates the possibility of your succumbing to auction fever and paying much more for an item than you wanted or intended to.

You probably associate the term "auction fever" with weak-minded souls who pay outrageous amounts for peculiar merchandise in a fit of especially acute mental aberration. Contrary to this supposition, auction fever can and usually does get almost every auctiongoer at some time or another. The kind of sale does not matter. Auction fever can make you bid $20 for a bowl worth $5 as fast as you bid $1,600 for a pair of famille rose vases worth $800. Auction fever defies exact definition. The nearest that I can come is that it is a mysterious something in the air that arouses the competitive and/or acquisitive instinct in a bidder. It strikes men and women, old and young with equal ferocity. It may or may not require a clever auctioneer to spread its infection. One of the most extreme examples that I've ever seen involved an auctioneer so inept that he could barely call bids, much less incite passion.

If we don't know the exact cause of auction fever, we certainly know its result: overpriced and sometimes eccen-

tric merchandise forever reminding us of our fecklessness. It is the auctiongoer who regularly suffers from this malady who comprises the large part of dissatisfied auction fans.

Most people brave the risk of auction fever because they feel more comfortable doing their own bidding. This certainly gives the auctiongoer more flexibility, allowing him to adjust his actions to the conditions of a particular sale, which are not always or even usually predictable in advance of the event.

There are hazards in bidding. In fact, the auctioneers to whom I spoke felt that, by and large, it was in the bidding that most auctiongoers slip up. A lot of auctiongoers, rather than following the bidding and going to their limit, start trying to guess who's bidding against them. Is it the house running up the bid? Is it some affluent, determined-looking person? Is it a well capitalized dealer? Even if you learn the answer, what good does it do you? There's certainly nothing that you can do about it save drop out of the sale, which is what the other bidders want anyway. Someone who's spent a lot of time on both sides of the block told me, "I don't even look at who's bidding against me. I don't care. I know what I'm going to pay."

While you are looking around, trying to spot the competition, the auctioneer may knock the item down to someone else. As for house bidding, there is equally little that you can do about this even if you suspect it, for it is almost impossible to second-guess a good auctioneer in the middle of a sale. He may be house bidding; he may be executing an absentee bid. This is why it is so important to go to the limit that you are willing to pay and then stop. One house that I suspect does a good bit of house bidding to push up prices will sometimes, I have noticed, back up. That is, if someone starts an old engraving for $10 and your final bid is $17.50, your limit on this item, the house may go on to $20, then when no other legitimate bidder comes in to top the $20, the auctioneer will look around and say innocently, "Now who gave me that $20 bid? Well, I know somebody did. We don't have all day, so I'll just take the $17.50. I believe that was yours, sir."

There is always the chance, of course, that you could

have quit bidding at $12.50 and gotten the engraving. On the other hand, at lower levels there is generally legitimate competition, so you would be taking the risk of losing the engraving as it is knocked down to someone else for $15.

For some reason, it comforts a segment of auctiongoers to hear the auctioneer announce that, "Everything is sold to the higest bidder at this house, regardless of price." Like those implied guarantees, this means nothing. What is to keep the highest bidder from being the consignor or the house acting in his behalf?

There is no way, short of ESP, that you can know what the other people involved in the auction intend to do, and you cannot logically base your buying decisions on what you think they may do. You can, however, decide what you are willing to do, then do it.

Therefore, rule number one for successful bidding is to *concentrate on the bidding* and the bidding alone. You've already looked at the merchandise; this is not the time to chat with your neighbors; this is not the time to dig into your purse or pockets for a cigarette. This *is* the time to watch the auctioneer and floor men as if they were mice and you a hungry owl.

Rule number two would seem to be to *bid decisively*. As one auctioneer remarked of a bid, "If I don't see it, I don't know it's there." Auctioneers are notoriously alert in recognizing bids. What a casual onlooker would take for a modest lowering of the eyes, the auctioneer may recognize instantly as a motion to bid. Still, you are in a much better position if you bid decisively because the auctioneer and floor men will pay closer attention to you.

There are few things more frustrating than losing something that you want very badly simply because the auctioneer did not see your tentative little gesture. As one auctioneer insisted, "The way to bid is then, there, and right now, and that's it." There are no possible mistakes, no chance of the auctioneer taking you twice. By taking you twice, I mean the practice that some auctioneers have of pretending to have recorded an intervening bid between the time that you began your slow motion bid and the time that you completed it. The bid may have been $20 at the instant you started bidding; by the time you finish—if you are slow—you may find yourself bidding $25.

This brings up the flip side of the coin. We have all heard the half-funny, half-horrible tale about the lady who waved to a friend at an auction and wound up owning a stuffed mongoose for $50. I have never seen this happen; I have never heard of it happening in real life. No doubt it does, so it is probably better not to be too free with your hands at auctions. Still, most auctioneers know the difference between a casual movement and a bid; if they have any doubt, they will usually ask you if you are bidding. If they knock an item down to you on the mistaken assumption that you have been bidding when you were not, they will—at least from my observation—generally honor your protest and resell the merchandise. Just remember they don't have to.

Rule number three is to *choose your approach to bidding and stick to it*. There are two categories of auctiongoers—those who act and those who react. We'll look at the reactors first.

I think of this school as the happenstance. Happenstancers usually go into an auction cold without paying much attention ahead of time to what is being sold. Likewise, they usually know little about the kind of merchandise being sold. If something interesting to them comes up in the course of the sale, they bid on it. How far they bid and the thought process that they employ during the bidding is strictly instinctive and usually emotional. They bid until they no longer want to bid, and where they want to stop depends on factors that have little to do with what is being sold. The only advice that I can give to those who prefer this approach is to sit as close as possible to the front of the auction so that you can at least see what you are bidding on and to stop bidding when you begin to feel uncomfortable because you'll probably feel a lot more uncomfortable if you continue.

The other school is more deliberate. The deliberators try to give the merchandise some inspection before the sale begins. They look harder at any specific item or items in which they are interested. They try to place a price on the item that is representative of its value to them and the use they intend for it. If there is a list for the auction, they usually mark their price beside the listed articles that interest them. Once the auction begins, they try to adhere to that price. Sometimes they get all the things that they want; sometimes none. Almost always, however, they suffer no later inward recriminations.

If you are a happenstancer, your time at auction may go like this:

Auctioneer: No. 48 on your list, a refinished rocker, turn-of-the-century kitchen style. Nice turnings. Look good in your den.

You: (Thinking) That is kind of nice, and it would look good in my den. I wonder what it'll go for?

Auctioneer: Will you start this lovely rocker at $20? $10 I have.

You: (Thinking) That's cheap. (Aloud) $12.50

Auctioneer: Thank you ma'am, $12.50. $12.50 I have, who'll make it $15? $15, thank you, sir. $17.50 anywhere?

You: (Thinking) That's still not too much. (Aloud) $17.50.

Auctioneer: $17.50, I have. $17.50. Who'll make it $20? $20 I have. $22.50 anywhere?

You: (Thinking) But that's more than he tried to start it for. Still, it would look good in the den. (Aloud) $22.50.

Auctioneer: $22.50, thank you. $25? $25? I have $25. Will you make it $27.50, ma'am?

You: (Thinking) That's a lot more than I thought it would go for. I just don't know if I like it that much. Still, it is pretty, and it'd be a shame to lose it now. (Aloud) $27.50.

Auctioneer: $27.50, I have. $27.50. $30? $30? $30? $30 in time, sir. A wise decision; this rocker is worth much more, an unusually fine specimen. Will you bid $32.50, ma'am? Be a shame to lose it now.

You: (Thinking) I don't know. $27.50 seemed like a lot, and now it's $32.50. I'm not sure if I like it that much, but I've gone this far. I might as well make this one last bid. I probably won't get it anyway. (Aloud) $32.50.

Auctioneer: $32.50, thank you. $35? $35? $35? $35, sir? $35 anywhere? then it is sold to the lady for $32.50, and her number is 16.

After the sale, one of three things will happen, almost inevitably. Your best friend will visit you, see the rocker, and reveal that her sister got one just like it last month at the thrift shop for $10. You will attend another auction and see a similar chair go for about the same amount you paid for yours. Or you will walk into the kickiest antique and junque shop in town and see a rocker just like yours, painted fire engine red, with a price tag of $125. You will be thrilled if you learn you've gotten a stupendous bargain, but you will probably be upset if you discover that you could have bought the same chair or something similar for much less. Pure luck is the only dividing line between the bargain and the extravagance.

If you are a deliberator, you will not enjoy the same pleasurable indecision as the happenstancer, and this might be typical of your auction routine:

To begin with, you arrive at the auction early enough to look over the merchandise. You spot an original drawing of the Art Nouveau period that you like and decide that it is worth $50 to you. You know that the drawing is probably more valuable than that, but that is all that it is worth to you.

The drawing is put up only ten minutes or so after the sale beings. The auctioneer says, "This is a beautiful, original drawing, very interesting subject matter, beautifully framed. Who will give me $100 for this drawing?"

You already know that you won't, so you sit there. Neither will anyone else, so the auctioneer drops the bid first to $50 then to $25.

When he says, "Well, will anyone give me $25", you quickly accept. You hope, of course, that he will get no advance, in which event the drawing is yours if the house does not require more than one bid to finalize a sale. Unfortunately, someone goes to $30. You immediately bid $35. You don't hesitate, don't ponder, don't try to second guess the other bidder or the auctioneer or anybody else. You know that it is possible to misgauge the pace of a sale so that the auctioneer will be in a hurry to move along and won't milk another bid.

The other bidder ups your $35 bid to $40. You at once bid $45; and while the auctioneer is fishing for the $50, you give that drawing another look and decide if you are willing to go over your $50 limit by even a few dollars should the other bidder agree to $50.

The auctioneer gets the $50 and turns to you. You indicate that you are willing to go $52.50, that being the amount of leeway you decided to allow yourself.

Having bid the $52.50, less than 10 percent over your predetermined limit, you are through with the bidding on this item.

If no one raises your bid, the drawing is yours at the price *you* decided was acceptable to you. If another bidder goes on, then you have lost the drawing. To continue bidding would violate your principle of keeping expenditures in line with an object's value to *you*.

Sticking with predetermined bid limits is difficult, especially at first. On occasion it may lead to some real regrets, but not as many as if you bid heedlessly onward (or based your decision to continue bidding on the auctioneer's estimate of the object's beauty, quality, or rarity). While there's a certain wistful pleasure in sitting before the fire on rainy nights and contemplating the ones that got away, there's nothing but rue in the overpriced item(s) sitting in your home to remind you daily of your abandon.

Establishing and sticking to predetermined top bids has another advantage: it keeps you from panicking during the sale and losing desirable merchandise by stopping short of what you were really willing to pay. I was with someone not long ago who wanted a certain Victorian silver teapot very much. She was willing to go to $75 on the sterling piece.

There didn't seem to be many people at the auction that night interested in silver. Several other silver items had gone very low, and my friend was continually decreasing in her mind the price that she would probably have to pay for what she was already thinking of as "her" teapot.

When it was put up, the auctioneer tried to get $100, dropped to $75, dropped to $50, then finally took my friend's $25 opening bid. She was ecstatic. The teapot started going up by $5's, and there were two other people bidding. When the price reached $50, my friend quit bidding. "The way it's going," she whispered, "it'll go for a lot more than $75, and I just don't see any point in helping to bid it up."

Almost immediately the teapot was sold for $55, as my friend sat there, angrily waiting for a competing bidder to up the price. She could possibly have had the teapot for $60. All the way home she moaned about it and complained, "I just *knew* it would go more."

Here we are again, and it bears repeating: *Never* try to second guess other bidders. Decide what you're willing to go for merchandise and go it without any undue delay or fuss. You are not only doing yourself a favor, but also extending a great courtesy to the rest of the audience, which does not get that much of a charge out of watching you scratch your head in indecision.

What you're willing to go for merchandise, of course, is entirely up to you and depends on your estimate of its value and your plans for it. If you are a dealer, you may be willing to buy anything going cheap because you can probably dispose of it for a profit in your shop. If you are a decorator, you may gauge the worth of an object in relation to its importance in the overall scheme of a project you are doing. If you are a serious collector, an item in your specialty will have a value to you different from its value to your neighbor who simply wants it for decorative purposes. If you are buying something for your house, you will probably be willing to spend more on something for the living room than the playroom. The point is to decide. Once you have decided, you are in control provided that you stick to your decision.

One of the fine arts of auctiongoing is waiting out the auctioneer. This takes a good idea of the real value of merchandise and a practiced eye for the auctioneer's temper and tempo. When the auctioneer begins by saying, "Who'll give me $50," he will usually drop to $40, to $30, or even to $20 if no one responds earlier. If there is still no response, he may drop further, but don't count on it. While you sit there, confidently expecting him to call for $10 or $15, he may say peremptorily, "Well, we might as well pass that; there's no interest." You can, of course, hurriedly interject a $20 bid, and he will usually keep the item on the block—but not always. Your $20 may have been far below a reserve price, and he may feel that there is not enough interest in the item to warrant putting it up again just because you were willing to bid $20 as an afterthought. Assuming that you do have a fairly good idea of values, you should be able to gauge an auctioneer's approach to opening bids and how far he is willing to go before passing an item. If you do not know values, then your best bet is to see what the auctioneer does on most of the items in the sale. If he will quarter his suggested opening bid before beginning to milk hard for a bid, then you know not to hesitate too long when an item he tried to start for $100 reaches the $25 point with no bid having been made. Here is one time when you really need to second guess the auctioneer if you plan on cutting your opening bid fine.

Whatever your approach to bidding, you can never know too much about the kind of merchandise that you are likely to be bidding upon. In fact, it is unlikely that you can ever know enough. In the first place, such an enormous variety of things comes up at auction that it would probably be impossible to know even a little about all of it. In the second place, auctions are supposed to be fun—not a return to the drudgery of lessons.

Having made this acknowledgment, I state unequivocally that the more an auctiongoer knows about merchandise, the happier he will be with the results of his auctiongoing.

There are people, including some quite intelligent types, who claim, "I don't care what I buy, as long as I like it, so it doesn't make any difference to me what it is." This proclamation of independence does not, I have observed, keep them from rushing hurriedly to a reference book to identify what they think they have bought nor from being bitterly disappointed when it turns out that they guessed wrong after all.

Most of the pros that I consulted, auctioneers and auctiongoers alike, emphasized the importance of research, not just in books but in museums, historic restorations, antique and junque shops, antique shows, flea markets—anywhere that one is likely to hear about or see a variety of the sort of merchandise that regularly shows up on the auction block.

"I think especially that anyone specializing in a certain field had better know his field before going to an auction," stressed one auctiongoing collector. "An auction can be an education, but not always to your good."

It is likely that when you start your auctiongoing career you are interested in acquiring a certain sort of item. If you go to auction to buy collectibles and are already knowledgeable in your field, then you are probably one up on the auctioneers and many of the other auctiongoers you will encounter, most of whom have only a general knowledge of merchandise. If you are not an experienced collector, however, you will probably have a happier time at auction if you will first read a book or two about what you want to collect and visit a few local shops to get an idea of the going retail prices. There are also several interesting magazines and newspaper-type publications to which you can subscribe that can be useful. For books that might be helpful to you, check the card catalogue at your public library under the name of the topic that interests you. You might also wish to consult the cards under the generic heading "Antiques" for general books that might contain information of use. For papers and magazines available, check with the library's periodical department. Even if the library doesn't stock the one that interests you (some of these publications are quite specialized), you can learn where to write for a subscription or further information. Also, in some areas,there are clubs which meet regularly to disseminate information about the collectible that interests the members.

On the other hand, if you are going to auction to pick up odds and ends for your house, your task is somewhat more complicated. If you know furniture periods and something about construction, you will be able to cope with buying furniture at auction until you reach the more expensive stages. If you do not know furniture, you will probably find it useful to buy a good book outlining characteristics of different furniture styles, something like Louise Ade Boger's *The Complete Guide to Furniture Styles*. Two small and inexpensive books that I have found invaluable are Thomas H. Ormsbee's *Field Guide to Early American Furniture* and *Field Guide to American Victorian Furniture*. Although the Ormsbee books are not new, they are still the best quick reference guides available, giving points of style and relative values in an easily usable format. When it comes to buying other articles for your house, you must learn to recognize quality and an object's potential usefulness to you.

Auction attendance counts as a very important part of research. After you have been to enough sales, you will find yourself groaning instinctively (with everyone else who knows) when the auctioneer describes a nineteenth-century Black Forest monstrosity of a desk as seventeenth-century Jacobean. Acquiring knowledge of old things, be they fine antiques or simply interesting whatevers, is often a process of osmosis in which you would be hard pressed to identify the moment when you recognized that something was or was not good of its kind.

The more you know about merchandise, the less likely

you are to succumb to the auctioneer's blandishments. You can remain unmoved by his pleading for an increase on an item on the basis of aesthetic or historic claims that you know or at least suspect that it does not merit.

Learning values is equally helpful and requires much the same sort of research. As you're looking at the merchandise in shops, for example, you can hardly help noticing the prices. Learning values is almost essential if you are collecting a specific sort of item and don't have unlimited funds.

The simplest way to keep abreast of values, which fluctuate rapidly at times, is to make a practice of visiting shops that carry the collectible and to read the publications that give current prices. If you're buying something more utilitarian—like a good-looking used stove or refrigerator—it helps to know the new price of a comparable model and to have a rough idea of possible repair charges should something be wrong with the used appliance. Usually, if asked point blank, the house will admit known defects.

While a knowledge of merchandise and values is admittedly not essential to happy auctiongoing, it does give you another big gun in the undeclared war between you and the person who holds the auctioneer's gavel.

Of course, all the forethought and knowledge in the world will not give you a great deal of protection against a dishonest auction house. A dishonest house can hurt you in several ways:

1. It can try to collect more than you bid on a particular item.
2. It can make very specific guarantees, then renege, so that your only recourse is a costly legal suit which the house is reasonably sure you will not bother to institute.
3. It can sell you one piece of merchandise, then substitute a similar item of inferior quality or condition.
4. It can short you on lots containing more than one item.
5. It can conspire with hired agents, sometimes local dealers, to run up prices (if it gets stuck with the merchandise, all it has to do is to run it through the sale again).

6. It can pretend to sell an item for an inflated price, setting a pace for similar items scheduled to follow.
7. It can buy whole loads of merchandise that it knows to be reproductions, then pass them off as old.

There are other tricks, but this should give you an idea of the possibilities for a resourceful and larcenous auction operator.

And there are larcenous operators. As one auction house proprietor admitted to me, "A lot of not too honest people are attracted to this business."

There is, of course, sometimes a fine line between illegal and merely dishonest; it is this line which determines if you have recourse to public authority should you feel cheated. Laws regarding auction house licensing and operation vary from area to area. One auction operator told me that you could count on lax laws almost invariably in a locale where auction houses had proliferated, especially if the proliferation were recent and rapid.

One cool auctioneer pointed out that many of the practices that the customers call dishonest are not, at least not within the framework of the house's terms by which all bidders agree to abide. Since most houses make no guarantee of condition before, during or after the sale, you will find it very hard to refuse payment for any item that was damaged after the sale was made if the house presses the matter. Also, the auctioneer has the final say on what your bid was, and you have usually agreed to this one-sided judgment by the mere fact of your having bid.

We discussed guarantees before, but it will not hurt to reiterate that they are generally meaningless. As for item substitution, how can you prove it? As a rule, only the suc-

cessful bidder truly remembers an item unless it is really spectacular. The same thing holds true for omissions from boxed merchandise when you pick the lot up after the sale. If you try to call the house's hand on a sale that you suspect was bogus, all the auctioneer has to do is to say that he has made a mistake and put the item up again. The sale of reproductions for antiques, especially prevalent today in the areas of glass and porcelain and certain more desirable items of furniture, is possible because few houses make legally binding guarantees as to the age, condition, or origin of what they sell.

How do you tell if a house is dishonest? If you think that a house has shorted or cheated you in some way, complain to the management as soon after the sale as possible. Don't complain just because you really wanted something and someone kept topping your bid. That could have been legitimate competition; and even if it were not, it would be difficult for you to prove any allegations. But if you have a solid complaint, take it to the management—the people who run the place. If they do not make it good or give you a satisfactory explanation, then you certainly have the right to wonder about their business tactics. If the same sort of thing happens again to you or to other auctiongoers at the same house, then you can be pretty sure that the house is at best careless and at worst crooked. Dishonesty or ineptness—when it comes down to it, what does it matter? Whatever the reason, that oil painting that you thought that you bought hangs somewhere else, not on your wall; the refrigerator that you thought was yours is cooling someone else's lettuce. The substitution or damage may have been inadvertent or premeditated, but the end result is the same—the customer has been had.

Let us say that you have decided beyond all doubt that a certain auction establishment is not honest in its dealings with its customers, what can you do short of getting a lawyer? According to the pros, very little.

Beginners, they point out, should always buy in a well established house where they can have confidence. They felt that a house that consistently practiced questionable ethics would not last long enough to become well established. The auctions that spring up like mushrooms, on the other hand, usually have little to lose in the way of good will, since they had none to begin with.

Even if you are an experienced auctiongoer, all our experts felt that your best protection against a dishonest house is to get out. In the final analysis, the sense of ethics of the people with whom you choose to do business does matter. Not even the oldest hand can be constantly on guard; and if you feel that you have to be, a lot of the fun disappears from the sale.

The professional conclusion seems to be that the terms under which most houses sell—be they printed, posted, stated, or implied—are so loaded in the house's favor that only its desire to maintain a reputable standing in the commercial community and to establish a continuing clientele keeps it honest. If the house already aspires to this goal, then you should have a reasonably good experience with it. If it does not, then there is little that the individual auctiongoer can do to change its way of doing business.

Chapter 10

Other Tips for Happy Auctiongoing

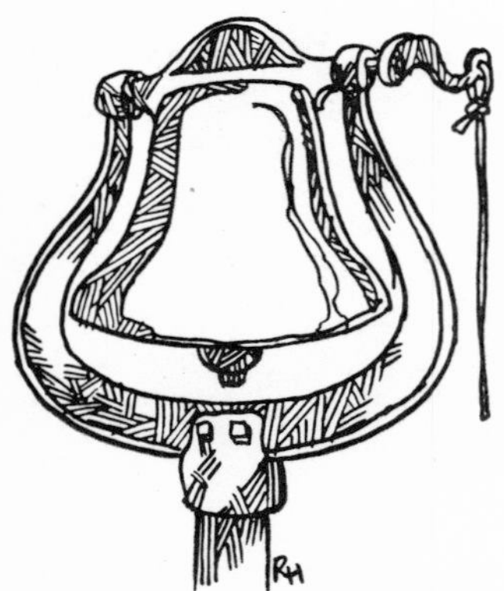

Standing outside the door of a country auction house not long ago was a well-dressed, prosperous-looking man handing out flyers. Bright yellow and red, they urged in bold type, "Let Madame Elsa tell your future, predict your love life, advise you in your business affairs."

He seemed to think that he was at the right place, and by now you may be wondering if you need Madame Elsa or someone like her to predict what will happen to you at auction. Will you be the victor who carries home the spoils, or will you be the spoils? In the long run, it is up to you, and you do not need to consult Elsa.

It is possible to get good—even spectacular—buys at auction. Everyone who knows auctions well agrees upon this. Not every sale contains an overlooked gem, but enough do to warrant the expectation. It is true that you are much more likely to wind up possessing the gem if you are either very lucky or if you have prepared yourself properly. If you feel that you were born holding a four-leaf clover, then you can skip the rest of this chapter. If, on the other hand, you tend to be a dropper of mirrors and a walker-under of ladders, you may find this advice helpful to one extent or another.

In the preceding chapter, we talked about the most common mistakes auctiongoers make and how to avoid some of them. This chapter summarizes miscellaneous bits of advice put forth by auction professionals, to wit:

1. What people should buy—whether furniture or what have you—is quality, workmanship, and rareness. If you buy with that in mind, you can't go wrong. Forget age; all age means is that something is old.
2. Do not buy at your first sale, but use the time to see how the auction works.
3. Learn the mechanics of the auction as well as possible, as they are what you must work with to buy.
4. Have confidence in your own judgment once you have some experience under your belt. I don't believe a lot of people who go to auctions know quality, and it's a mistake for an auctiongoer who does to let the apathy of an uneducated crowd make him uncertain of his own opinion of an item.
5. At auction you get better buys on higher quality merchandise. In an auction of 150 people, it's hard to get two people who want the really good things.
6. You have a very good chance of making a spectacular find at auction, but the odds are against it if you don't know what you're doing in the first place.
7. If you don't inspect the lot well enough ahead of time, you don't really know what you're bidding on, which can be an expensive way of playing blind man's bluff.
8. Buying really top quality antiques at auction is a risky business unless you qualify as an expert.

9. If you want to see what dealers think the coming wave will be, watch what they buy.
10. Never stop studying what you are doing. Use the auction as you would a school; keep track of what you are doing. Grade yourself if you like.
11. Remember your auction manners. There is a fine line between acceptable repartee between auctiongoer and auctioneer and outright boorishness. When in doubt, shut up. The auctioneer has his own way of getting back.
12. If the advertising is poor, the weather bad, and several other shows scheduled at the same time or even on the same day, you are likely to get better buys than you would otherwise.
13. Do not be discouraged by your failures. You can learn more from them, and in a way that you are more likely to remember, than from your successes—which are often pure luck anyway, so have little to teach you.
14. Remember that the auction is a business transaction and use the same common sense that you would apply to other business transactions.

With all of these neat-sounding bits of wisdom—which I admit are easier to record than to follow at all times—we will now progress to some specifics. Obviously, it is impossible to cover everything tricky in merchandise, as the auction includes such a variety of quality, condition, and kind. Following, however, are random comments on some fairly common pitfalls in the auction of average quality:

1. Watch out for the loose description "Chippendale ball-and-claw feet." In the first place, there is not a ball-and-claw foot in the entire *Director*, Chippendale's famous pattern book. In the second place, such feet have been tacked onto different pieces and styles of furniture since the 1730s. Most of the ball-and-claw footed furniture at auction today is of 1910 vintage or later.
2. Most auctioneers know very little about

woods. Everything is oak or walnut or mahogany or cherry, according to its finish (which signifies nothing) and whatever wood is most popular at the moment. If you care about the wood of which the item is made, don't take the auctioneer's word alone.

3. Many of the "new antiques" (after 1900, often after 1920) becoming so common at auctions have little intrinsic value because they are not well made, but they are big at the moment because of the nostalgia fad so that people are paying premium prices for the more unusual items.
4. Majolica ware has been made for centuries, and some designs and patterns have been reproduced many times. A lot of new majolica looks old because of an excellent antique finish.
5. Any porcelain or other merchandise bearing the name of the country of origin probably

dates after 1890 (to comply with the portion of the McKinley Tarriff Act requiring that this information be shown on all items imported into the U.S.). This does not mean, however, that all items so marked are after this date, nor does it indicate that all items not so marked are earlier.

6. Closed trunks or unopened boxes may contain wondrous treasure, or they may be full of rotted linens. This is strictly a gambler's game.
7. New farm bells are being sold for old at many auctions. Haulers buy them unpainted, then cover them with salt water so that they'll rust quicker. Then the bells are sold as old for almost twice what they would bring new. This same trick is also being pulled on reproduction iron banks and toys, now big collector's items.
8. Old buttons and badges, especially those featuring catchy advertising matter or political slogans, are being reproduced; and this merchandise is sometimes being sold as old. Ditto for old advertising trays and calendars.
9. When the auctioneer insists on selling something stacked or folded, there is usually a reason for it—one that will not make you happier with what you've bought when you unfold or unstack it later.

10. Chairs and couches with a lot of upholstery don't go well as a rule, even when the upholstery is in usable condition, so that it is possible to get good buys here if you like the fabric or are capable of redoing the piece yourself.
11. In almost every sale, the best merchandise will sell for much less than its real worth, the worst for much more.
12. When the house sells in groups, individual pieces of better quality or greater interest may get lost in the junk of a big lot. A treasure may be hidden in the midst of outlet store rejects, so always look carefully at such lots.
13. When a set of dishes is up and only one piece is shown around, make sure that *it* matches the rest. Sometimes the floor man will show an individual piece that looks like or at least is similar to the rest of the set, but is actually of much better quality. This is particularly common when the pattern of the dishes is one that has been reproduced many times over the years.
14. Look very carefully at eighteenth-century furniture in mint condition if what you want is a piece of this furniture. It is very rare for any furniture two hundred years old to be mint, and it is quite likely that you are looking at a "married" piece. This means that bits and pieces of two or more items of furniture have been neatly reassembled and refinished into a new and different item of furniture. As one auction house operator said, "Sure, maybe every piece in there is from eighteenth-century furniture, but it isn't a piece of eighteenth-century furniture."
15. Try to ascertain if a silhouette is a print or is actually cut. If cut, it is worth much more money.
16. Look at broken or cracked items with a realistic eye, keeping in mind your own facilities for

repair. Also, remember that—despite what the auctioneer may say—some of the pieces may be missing, enormously complicating the process of renewal.

17. In a similar vein, keep in mind that what you see is what you get. If the bed rails are missing, the finial gone, the lid to the teapot absent, you should not count on getting them later from the house even though the auctioneer or floor man may insist that the missing part is "in the back". It may or may not be and they may or may not be able or willing to find it later; but you have bought the imcomplete item no matter what.
18. There are people about who are capitalizing on the popularity of certain makes of porcelain by putting false marks on the backs of similar but inferior porcelain. R.S. Prussia red star is a particular favorite of the forgers, and sometimes they don't even bother to spell Prussia right.
19. Victorian cruet sets are becoming popular; but it is unusual to find one with all its bottles and stoppers in perfect condition. So when you see a "complete" cruet, make sure that all the pieces match and are intact. Usually they are not, and replacements that match are extremely difficult to locate. Also, if all the pieces do match, are they the same age as the frame or have they been newly bought and put in the container?
20. Old fashion prints are being reproduced and are not usually marked as reprints. Framed, these prints are very difficult to detect as reprints. If their age matters to you, be wary about the price.
21. The same thing is true of dated prints of any kind. Just because a tiny date appears at the lower left or right side of an engraving or etching does not mean that this is the date of *this*

engraving or etching. It is merely the date of the original. This version could have been run off last month provided the subject matter and artist are popular enough to warrant the trouble.

22. Always assume that clocks won't work because they usually won't, and few houses will guarantee them—even houses that will offer some guarantees on other merchandise.
23. Watch for the term "age line" in the auctioneer's spiel. It can mean anything from a barely perceptible line to a bad crack.
24. When the auctioneer says Wedgwood and the mark on the bottom says Wedgwood, it

doesn't always mean the Wedgwood that you think. (There have been at least a dozen companies using the name or some variation thereof.) Ditto for certain other names or marks that have gained such wide acceptance either in the past or today that later firms were tempted to capitalize on the name. Your best protection if you collect the works of a certain manufacturer is to memorize the firm's marks.

25. The numbers on porcelain marks do not usually refer to the date of the piece's manufacture or even the pattern's inception, but to the date of the company's founding or the model number of the item.
26. On fancy frames, look closely to see if there is any bad damage that has been disguised by a new coat of gilding. In fact, give a suspicious eye to any frame that has obviously been recently painted or gilded. Usually there was a good reason for the coverup, as most people don't monkey around with frames as long as they are in acceptable condition.
27. Check dusty chair and table legs to see if they're cracked.
28. Be wary of buying shaving mirrors or dressing mirrors that are not assembled, as sometimes the mirrors won't fit the frames with which they have been put up.
29. Crazing will sometimes bleach out of earthenware (with a little Clorox) if it is severe enough to bother you.
30. Many of the lamps and chandeliers and lanterns that come up have European wiring that will not work with American electrical systems. When you buy this kind of merchandise, keep in mind the expense of having the wiring replaced.
31. When a work of art is under glass, it is sometimes hard to distinguish a good print from a

watercolor or even a smooth oil, and auctioneers have been known to make mistakes.

32. An ugly or damaged frame will usually drag down the price of even a good picture, so if you have a good frame supplier, you can get some real bargains here.
33. Remember that you may have to remove any merchandise that you buy yourself and decide if really big or heavy items are good or cheap enough to warrant the expense and trouble.
34. If you have a specific question about the condition of what is on the block, ask it. If cornered, the auctioneer or floor man will usually admit damage that he would not point out voluntarily.

This could go on indefinitely, but I think that you have the idea by now. Auctiongoing is not some esoteric process, but rather a business activity with component parts that are open to analysis and judgment.

As early as possible in your auctiongoing career, you should decide what you hope to gain. Quite obviously, the dealer must view auctions differently than must the private collector; the regulars have a different outlook than the person who attends once a year to buy Christmas gifts; the pleasure seeker requires something different from a sale than the person intent on buying a certain kind of merchandise. The important thing is that you should decide what you want from this oddly appealing combination of commercialism and entertainment.

If going to auctions does not render you some positive good, then you should not go. Auctions are simply a pastime where it is possible for you to gain certain desired advantages. It is an inescapable fact that if you want to come away from the auction satisfied, then *you* must establish and adhere to your own criteria for satisfaction.

Chapter 11

Auction Addiction

Auction addiction is a condition or—if you prefer—a state of being in which the auctiongoer begins to crave the auction as the glutton yearns for the eight-course meal. As is so often the case with the victuals of the glutton, the kind of auction becomes increasingly less important and the merchandise purchased more a by-product than the primary reason for going to a sale. It is the act of attending the auction that enchants the addict, and he can no more ignore the allurements of the hall than a small boy can walk around a sand pile.

Quite simply, the auction addict would rather go to an auction than do anything else. You know that you are addicted when:

The first part of any newspaper you look at is the section of the Classifieds where auctions are advertised.

You know the Terms of Sale better than the auctioneer at almost any auction you attend.

You've forgotten how to read a retail price tag.

You come back from your first trip to Europe talking about Christie's, Sotheby's, Paul Brandt, Palais Galliera, and the Galerie Koller instead of Westminster Abbey and the Eiffel Tower.

You pass up the chance to see a hit play free, with your best friend to go to an auction with someone you really don't like very much.

You are incapable of driving by a sign that says, "Best auctions in the world! Ask here for directions." Even if the sign is scrawled in blue marking pencil on warped cardboard and "here" is a dilapidated service station.

Pass is something done by an auctioneer, not a quarterback.

You are at your most comfortable in an uncushioned, straight-backed chair with the auctioneer crying, "The sale is underway."

You find yourself thinking in terms of a bigger house or apartment because there is no room to put anything else.

Your garage looks like a Rube Goldberg Happening that didn't come off.

You never buy anything in a store without feeling guilty.

You picked up this book because force of habit was too strong to resist the call.

Now that we've uncovered the addict, let's look at what made him that way. Some addicts seem born to auctions as salmon are born to swim upstream. From the first moment they enter the charmed circle and seat themselves within range of the auctioneer's hypnotic stare and pleading voice, they are lost. Never again can their friends count on them for bowling every Tuesday night; there may be a special sale one Tuesday. Never again can their spouses count on an uncluttered garage or attic; while the addict usually does not buy much, if any, at most sales, a certain amount of stuff is bound to pile up over the years as if by gravitational pull. Never again need the addict wonder what to do with that excess money in the checking account; there will not be any. Many lives are changed by the born addict's happening upon his intended fate, not least of all his own.

For every born addict, there are probably several created by circumstances. What can turn an otherwise normal person into an auction hound? A lot of things, including:

Buying a box of junk pottery for half a dollar and finding buried in it an early nineteenth-century creamer worth $25. Substitute a piece of beatup furniture for a dollar or two that turns out to be suspected Duncan Phyfe worth whatever you can get for it or some other equally fortuitous turn of luck, and you have a tale that appears time and again in the history of most auction addicts.

Happening on an auctioneer who combines the charm of Cary Grant, the wit of Will Rogers, and the appeal of a pre-Yoko Beatle.

Moving so close to a good auction house that it seems silly not to go to the sales.

Seeing something that you bought in a store last week for $24.95 go for $7.50 at auction.
Watching your friends drool with envy over that unusual lamp you bought at auction for about a tenth of what they think it cost.
Getting for $10 a steel box full of assorted hand tools worth $75.
Finding the dessert forks to match your grandmother's silver, which has been out of stock for forty years.

Personally I see nothing wrong with being an auction addict provided that food is not actually snatched from the mouths of one's family to feed the habit. There are much worse addictions, though none perhaps tending to so much bulk. There are people, however, who find their affliction as irritating as it is stubborn, and they have experimented with cures.

One determined woman said that she tried to go to so many sales that she would become sick of them. Another confessed that she had tried buying the worst item in a sale in the hope that all this junk sitting around the house would discourage her. A man claimed that never going to any auction that required less than one hour's driving time —preferably in bad traffic—had helped him. The man sitting next to him said a good trick was to alienate the auctioneer at your favorite house, then you'd be ashamed to go back. A friend told me that her cousin had actually tried self-hypnosis to convince herself of the senselessness of being drawn to the hall whenever its doors opened.

Do the cures work? I don't really think so since most of the people who talked about them were interviewed at auction.

Some people do lick the habit, but it seems to be a matter of luck, not planning. "One day I just didn't want to go anymore," an ex-addict explained. "I still attend an occasional sale with a friend, but it's nothing special anymore." She said this sadly, as you or I might speak of an old love whose unique attraction we have forgotten.

Although I made no survey of addicts, near-addicts, or

ex-addicts, I rather suspect that the first two categories outnumber the last. In any event, here are the case histories of five actual auctiongoers in various stages of addiction.

Case History No. 1
The Incubative Addicts

John and Janice C. are an attractive and articulate young couple with a happy marriage, a five-year-old son, a miniature Schnauzer, and an appealingly offbeat approach to life. They live in a two-story brick townhouse in a new luxury complex only minutes away from the heart of a large Southern city.

Neither John, an artist, nor Janice, a young businesswoman, has ever felt the inclination or the need to study interior design or decorative periods; but in their case, this indicates not indifference to their surroundings, but rather a positive instinct for what is right for them. Basically it was this instinct that led them to auctions in the first place.

"We'd heard some friends talking about auctions and were intrigued with the idea that we could find some really different things at good prices. In fact, we thought about going for months before we actually attended our first auction," John confessed. "Then we moved into this townhouse, which is much larger than our apartment had been, and suddenly we found that for the first time we had more room than furniture."

"It was the dining room that really set us off," Janice put in. "We'd never had a separate dining room before, and we didn't have anything to put in it. We looked in all the better furniure stores and found out that we would have to pay a small fortune to get something that we'd really like to live with. Besides, we didn't like the idea of knowing that anything we bought new was likely to turn up in the homes of our friends or even the house down the street. We wanted something different."

"It was really fantastic," John continued. "The first trip we made to the auction galleries to look over the things that were going up was the day that we found exactly what we liked for the dining room. It was a group of furniture in the

Jacobean style, which we learned was probably made in the 1920s; its construction was careful and sturdy. There was a refectory table, a court cupboard, a small server, a sideboard, and six chairs. To begin with, the table was what we liked most, and we were determined to get that if nothing else."

Their auctiongoing friends assured them that similar sets had sold at this particular auction house for as little as $250 and that certainly they wouldn't have to go more than $450 for the entire set. Each of the items was scheduled to be put up separately; and since John and Janice were determined to be practical about their first auction experience, they decided ahead of time the limit to which they were willing to go on each of the items. The table was their favorite, and they set a generous limit of $175 on it. A little uncertain of auction procedure, they asked their auction-hardened friends to come along and bid for them. So certain were they of getting the set at their price (a maximum of $475 for the lot), that they spent the time before the sale discussing just where each piece would go. But one of those quirks of fate that seem to dog auctions materialized in the form of an impulsive bride who coveted the same furniture.

As their friends prepared to bid for them, John and Janice watched nervously. The eager bride opened with a $100 bid for the table and chairs, whch the auctioneer had decided to put up together. John and Janice were not too happy about this as they did not like the chairs, but they were determined to have the table. The bidding quickly reached the $175 limit that they had set on the table alone, and John nudged his friend to keep bidding. The bid went to $250, to $275, to $300, to $350, to $375. Then it was the girl's turn. The auctioneer fixed his persuasive gaze on her and intoned, "It's your last chance. Will you go $400?" As if mesmerized, she mutely nodded yes.

"It nearly killed us, but we decided that we didn't want the table that much," John said. "We debated whether to bid on the remainder of the set when it came up, and decided that we would only if the price were right." It was. They got the court cupboard for $50, the large sideboard for $55, and the small server for $55. The bride had wanted these pieces too, but she had blown her budget on the table and chairs, giving them little competition.

It was not with a great deal of enthusiasm that John and Janice left their first auction. Not getting the table had been a big disappointment. What salvaged the experience for them was getting their acquisitions home and polished. Their "new" furniture was in excellent condition and was perfect for their dining room. It had cost them only a fraction of the retail tab for comparable new furniture. They debated whether or not to wait for future auctions to find their table and chairs, but the press of a planned series of visits from distant relatives made them decide to turn to the antique shops, where they found a refectory table they liked more and chairs that were of much better quality and more pleasing appearance than the lot for which they had bid the same amount of money at auction.

Now their dining room is anything but empty. Red velvet curtains over French doors are a perfect foil for the burnished sheen of the dark furniture. A crystal and brass chandelier sparkles overhead, and large plants in the corners provide a pleasant contrast to the room's casual elegance.

What did they think of their first auction experience?

"We loved it!" Janice exclaimed. "We were thrilled with what we got, especially at the price." "I learned not to rent an eighteen-foot powerlift truck to pick up three pieces of furniture," John grinned. "But the furniture looked a lot bigger at the auction than it did in that truck. It gave the guys at the auction house a good laugh. That's one of the things I don't like about most auctions—the fact that they don't deliver the big stuff. Sometimes it isn't very convenient to get a truck or trailer."

"And I don't like the idea of something that you really want getting away," Janice continued. "At least in a store, the price is marked on the merchandise; if you want the item, you just pay the price. But at an auction there could be someone there who is really determined to get whatever it is that you want. Like the table that night. And if they've got the money, they can run the thing up way above what it's actually worth and maybe so high that you can't bid against them. It's a very frustrating feeling to know that there's a good chance that you might lose something that you really want."

In spite of these drawbacks, both of them agreed that they like auctions. "They're great," Janice enthused, her dark eyes shining. John agreed, adding, "It's the suspense and curiosity of what certain pieces will bring."

"I think it's fun to see what everybody else bids on," Janice laughed. "Yeah," concurred John. "And have you ever noticed that if there's one particular thing you really like, everyone at the auction gives it the eye and checks its number and talks about it? But when the thing comes up for sale, hardly anyone will bid. It's interesting to see that what we go for isn't usually what anybody else wants, at least not enough to bid on it."

"Maybe that's because what we want is usually odd," Janice pointed out. "You know, another thing I like about auctions is that there isn't any temptation to charge any-

thing. I guess you could because I've seen Master Charge signs around at some of the sales, but somehow I'm never tempted to charge. At auction I buy it, and I pay for it. I like that feeling of not waiting for bills to come in. Auctions have changed my thinking about several things. Stores, for instance. Going to auctions has completely changed the way I feel about shopping in retail stores for certain kinds of things. I go in and look around, but then decide that I'll wait and have the fun of watching for whatever it is that I want at auction. That way I might be able to get something completely different from what I can find in the stores and maybe spend less money for something that's really better. Of course, I still buy some things in stores. I'd be cautious about buying, say, an appliance at an auction, or upholstered furniture. You could wind up with a big repair bill."

"I wouldn't want to buy any furniture that was rough," John agreed. "I don't have that much room to work on anything, and I'd really have to want something to buy it in bad condition."

What about auctions producing good buys?

"I'd have to say sometimes," John answered. "It's like anything else; you have to be careful about what you're doing. But the possibility of good buys definitely exists. In the long run, you have to weigh just what this specific thing is worth to you in terms of usefulness or decoration."

Their buying philosophies differ.

John said, "Usually I go with something specific in mind, which is not to say that I might not buy something on impulse, but usually not."

"That's no fun," Janice protested to her bearded husband. "I'd rather see something that I like and find a use or a place for it."

"I know, I know," John groaned.

As might be expected from an artist with a strong streak of practicality, John's primary interest in auctions is twofold: the opportunity to find an appealing article that may be one of a kind and the chance to acquire something that he can use at a price below, sometimes far below, current retail values for a comparable article. "But once I get what I've bought home," he confessed, "I begin to wonder about the thing itself. Who had it before and what they were like and how they used it. There seems to be a story in everything old if you take the time to think about it."

In John and Janice's home, there are many stories. Old circus posters prove compatible companions for John's very sophisticated oils and graphics. In the living room a nineteenth-century pine pie safe with a screened front holds books and small collectibles—old and new—in its lighted interior. The pie safe's honest simplicity of line and wood provides a highly effective foil for the tufted black vinyl couch and love seat which wrap around two sides of a square mock-tortoise shell coffee table topped by groups of delicately colored, one-of-a-kind mushrooms through whose ranks tiny ceramic snails march. In a corner, near the modern fireplace, sits a square armchair upholstered in black and white plaid linen. From over the fireplace a binomial clock that John invented serves a dual function as timekeeper and *objet d'art*. In the daytime, opaque white fabric curtains the windows, affording bright light to the interior and making it as gay as the old circus that its posters advertise. At night, when the windows are covered by heavy red velvet drapes and a log fire glows on the hearth, all the things that John and Janice have collected so painstakingly combine in the warm, dim light to make the room appear a highly personalized cave into which to settle comfortably and relax.

Now that their house is slowly filling up with all the things, big and small, that transform space into a home, do they intend to continue going to auctions?

"Yeah," John said resignedly. "Or at least as often as we can."

"I think mainly we'd be looking for smaller decorative things . . . " began Janice.

"And furniture, maybe a wardrobe for the bedroom," John broke in.

"And whatever strikes our fancy," Janice laughed. "I guess, really, we're just getting hooked on auctions. It really grows on you, doesn't it? I enjoy all of it, even the suspense of whether or not we'll get what we went for. It's like a game."

"It's like Christmas," John corrected. "Like anticipating what Santa Claus will bring you when you're a kid. Every trip to the display rooms is like looking forward to Christmas. It's like, what did they bring us this week?"

Does it bother them that one day their own treasured belongings might well wind up on the auction block?

John grinned wickedly, then answered, "No, it doesn't bother me at all. It gives me kind of an ego trip. How about you, Janice?"

"Our stuff at an auction—wow!"

CASE HISTORY NO. 2
The Seasoned Addicts

Annette B. is a history teacher in a large city high school. Her husband Ken is an aerospace engineer employed by one of the giants of the industry. They are young, energetic, and very much in control of their marriage, their careers, and their lives. Together they share that rare combination of qualities: common sense and the willingness to experiment. Their approach to life reflects both, so that in retrospect auctiongoing seemed inevitable for them.

"It was the fault of some ex-friends of ours," Ken joked. "No, seriously, they're still friends, but they did take us to our first auction. That was over two years ago."

And what was Ken's reaction to that first sale?

"We didn't go to another one for months."

"There was a huge difference in prices between that first sale and most of the others we've gone to," explained Annette. "But that was because of the kinds of things that were being sold that first night. There were some really good things, but the prices were unbelievable."

"We were a little disappointed at the prices naturally," Ken reiterated, "because we'd heard a lot about the good buys at auctions. Apart from the prices, I did have another very definite reaction to that first auction. After all the indoctrination with the tobacco auctioneers in the ads on the tube, I was surprised that I could actually understand the auctioneer at once."

Ken and Annette's pleasant, spacious home in an old town now being engulfed by a rapidly growing city contains

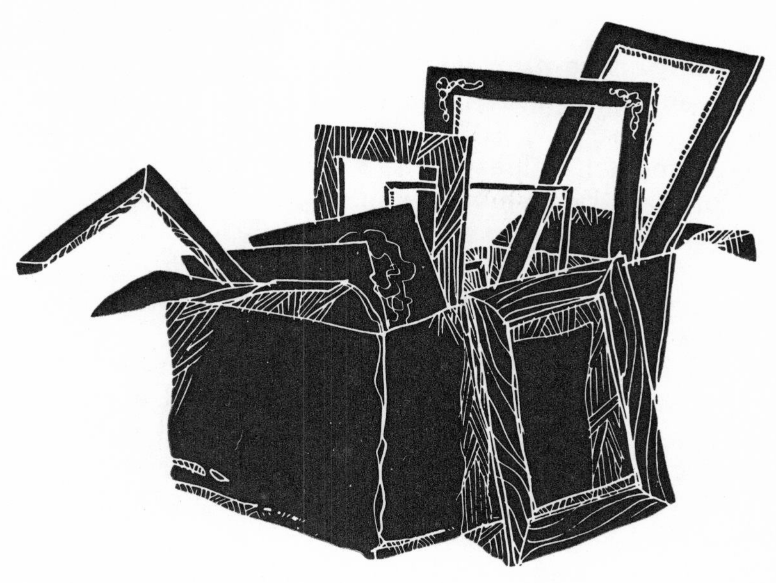

constant decorative surprises. In the living room, for example, an elegant, modern sofa of gold crushed velvet sits comfortably in the midst of turn-of-the-century oak furniture, stained dark. A downstairs bedroom sports twin hospital beds (great for watching TV or reading in bed because of the adjustable backs). Everywhere there are pictures of all kinds: nineteenth-century engravings framed by Ken in sumptuous gold and velvet; old lithographs; original watercolors. In the blue and white dining room, heavy dark pine furniture shows off blue and white ironstone. An old metal log holder sits in the small fireplace. Unusual early irons are scattered everywhere. A zither sits on a desk in the study. Around every corner there is something always interesting, often beautiful, and usually different. All of these things combine to create a distinctly individualistic aura for this highly charged young couple.

It is clear that little of their decorating budget has been spent in retail stores. When asked, they said that, yes, many of their very favorite things been bought in antique or junque shops or at auction, mostly at auction.

Of the dozens of articles that they have bought at auction in the past two years, the one which pleases them most is the largest—an impressive, turn-of-the-century secretaire in beautifully grained and detailed oak and in perfect condition. It cost only $275. Other buys with which they have been specially pleased are a competently executed watercolor of an English village, nicely framed, for only $11 and a French-style night stand on cabriole legs that needed only polishing and cost $10.

Have they bought anything at auction that they regretted?

"Gee," Annette said, "we buy things at such a low cost compared to new that it doesn't matter if we were a little disappointed or if whatever we bought that night wasn't perfect."

"I regret buying that heavy onyx mantel clock," Ken remembered. "It's in the basement right now."

"We can always put it in a garage sale," Annette sighed. "He bought things that if we had reflected ahead of time we wouldn't have bought because of the price. Like that wall clock for $55." She pointed to a handsome Victorian wall clock hanging in the living room.

"That second Windsor chair I didn't like for $90," Ken put in, indicating a prime example of the English Windsor sitting under the disputed clock. "You bought that out of stubbornness."

"Yes," Annette admitted, "but two of them had already gone that night, and I couldn't touch them. I was determined to get it. And you have to admit it was a good buy at shop prices."

Have there been many items that they have since regretted not buying at auction?

"Some paintings and things that I didn't appreciate or need at the time—it was before we bought the house," Annette remembered.

"And a few chests that went low for their quality about the same time as the pictures," Ken recalled.

Is there anything that they wouldn't buy at auction, generally speaking?

"I definitely wouldn't buy an appliance at an auction," Annette said positively. "And I would be afraid to buy material and records."

"Anything with cloth," Ken agreed. "Too, I'm wary of veneered furniture. You can get into some problems with that. Anthing electronic. Anything that I don't have the capability of repairing myself."

Obviously both of them are enamoured of what you can find at auction, so it was interesting to see what they thought about the auction itself.

"One thing that bothers me," Annette began, "is that you bid in an emotional state. At least, I do. And I get more emotional satisfaction in comparing prices and values and reflecting, but there simply isn't time to do this at auctions and the whole atmosphere is against the effort anyway. There's always a feeling of emotion."

"The psychology of the thing is the brief emotional encounter with the object," Ken pointed out. "If you don't buy it, that's it. Still, the price is usually better at auction."

"To me," he continued, "the worst thing about auctions is that you have to sit and wait while they sell all this junk, if it's a bad sale, while you wait for whatever it is that you came for. Of course, the boredom thing is a part of the psychology."

"You're so relieved when something halfway decent comes up in the middle of a bad auction that you find your-

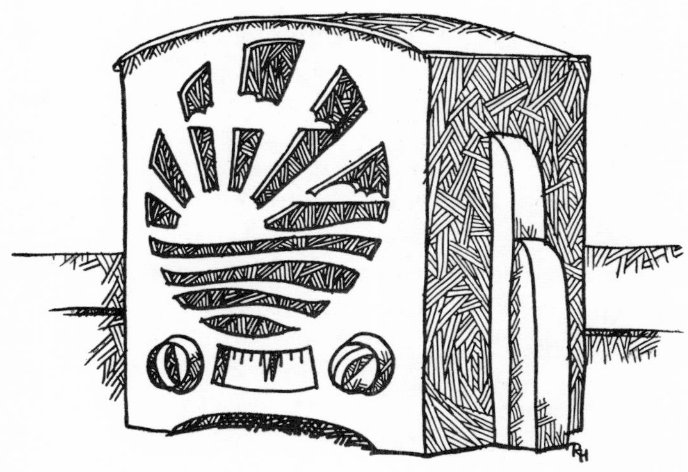

self bidding on it, especially if the price is low, just out of relief,'' Annette agreed.

''Too, I don't like it when the auctioneer starts bugging the crowd about not paying enough. Sometimes it's funny; but if he goes on long enough, it's irritating. A mild irritation, but an irritation,'' Ken added.

Basically, what do they like about auctions? Their answers were almost identical, which may explain why they continue auctiongoing in a happy frame of mind.

''The good values and the constant parade of something different,'' Ken said.

''Yes,'' Annette continued, ''and the curiosity, the novelty.''

''Of course, there's that other great factor—the laughs,'' Ken said.

When asked if they had any special approach to auctions, they shook their heads.

''We don't go ahead of auction to inspect the merchandise because it's logistically impossible as a rule,'' Ken explained.

Do they ever try to research any article that they see in advance on the rare occasions when they can view a lot in advance?

''No, because we don't buy at all for antique value,'' Ken said.

''So it is irrelevant to us that something is what they claim,'' Annette emphasized. ''We buy because we like it. I would be curious about it afterwards, if at all.''

''It's a nice fringe benefit if you know,'' Ken conceded. ''You can have the fun of telling someone who asks. But that's all.''

What do they think of antiques, even the new antiques, as an investment?

''Hands down, they're a better investment than, say, new furniture, especially cheaper new furniture,'' Ken declared.

''But I wouldn't go into it that way,'' Annette broke in. ''It's too much of a burden. You'd have to be too knowledgeable as a beginner.''

They have noticed several disturbing trends since they've been going to auctions.

"It generally seems as if everything is going higher," Annette thought.

"The mechanical-type junk is especially higher," Ken said sadly, for he loves gadgetry of all kinds, especially if it is primitive. "And the crowds have definitely increased. Much thicker crowds, at least at the places that we go to."

"Yes," Annette agreed, "a lot more people. Sometimes it's standing room only where there used to be empty chairs."

Even so, both of them said that they would recommend auctions to young people as a good source for house or apartment furnishings.

"I think a good tip for people who want to buy at auctions is for them to look in both new and used furniture stores to get a good idea of price comparisons," Ken suggested.

"Auctions are a great way for people to start furnishing their homes, especially if they don't have much money to begin with," he continued. "But it might precipitate some divorces."

"Auctions can lead to fights," Annette explained. "We don't always want the same things, and our buying philosophies differ. If I like something for itself, I'll find a place for it."

"When we were in the apartment, you wouldn't believe how many hours we spent arranging the furniture and even the pictures on the walls to fit something else in!" Ken remembered.

In spite of this occasional disagreement, do they plan to heed the auctioneer's chant in the future? In answer they both laughed weakly.

Annette passed the buck. "This one's yours."

"Sure we'll go," Ken said. "There'll be a certain basic list of replacement-type items. A trend toward finer things, maybe a bit more toward the formal stuff. Other than that, probably higher-type miscellaneous items. but no collections of anything. We don't want a collection. It's too much trouble to learn all that you need to know, and storage can be a big problem."

His moustache quivering with amusement, Ken willingly complied with the request to describe an auction: "A group of itchy-nosed people sitting around a cemetery bantering about buying the bones. Because that's what it boils down to."

And one gets the feeling that he and Annette will probably be sitting on the tombstone in the center of the front row.

Case History No. 3
The Confirmed Addict

Grace R. is an attractive widow in her mid-sixties. She lives in a neo-Georgian House on a quiet, shady street in a good suburb of a large city on the Atlantic coast. Growing up in New England, she went to her first auction as a baby in her father's arms.

"At least, that's how the family story goes," she laughed. "And I can't remember a time when I didn't go to auctions. My husband and I went even on our honeymoon!"

It is in vain, however, that one looks around her well furnished study for the usual signs of such enduring attendance. Here there is no hodge-podge of items, each individually clamoring for attention, but a harmonious setting for this pleasant woman's active life. From this room she handles the details of her volunteer office work for several charities; and it is here that she keeps up with her large, world-wide circle of correspondents. It is a working room whose muscles are sheathed in serenity, but are nonetheless present. There is a large desk: "It's a Regency partners' desk and has an amazing amount of storage space." A sturdy, oversized canterbury substitutes successfully for a file cabinet for current projects: "I bought that at a little shop in London years ago; it's one of the few things in this room that didn't come from auction. That Turkish rug came from a gallery sale in New York. I found the majolica pot that doubles as a wastebasket at a house auction in Pennsylvania. The hand-colored etchings of the Dickens' characters came from an ante-bellum mansion in a little town in Alabama: I happened on that sale by accident, I remember. The platters hanging on either side of the windows came from different sales on Cape Cod. Most of the rest of the furnishings came from gallery or country sales in the Southeast

"I guess the oldest thing—in terms of when I got it—is that gilt-framed mirror over the mantel. I bought it in, I think, 1928. The newest is the silver-gilt inkstand on the desk; I found it at a gallery sale just last month."

As she spoke I looked closely at the room. Any of the things in it might or might not have been striking on its own. It is plain that they have been carefully chosen and arranged to fit Grace's basic concept of her life. The effect is luxurious, but subtle; lovely, but practical. When I remarked how smoothly all the things in the study worked together, she nodded gracefully that, yes, she supposed they did.

"I know I certainly enjoy this room, so I suppose it does work. Of course, I'm very particular about what I put in here. It's my favorite room, and I spend a great deal of time here."

Was the rest of her house furnished at auction?

"For the most part. The couches in the living room we had made. Some of the lighting fixtures were bought retail. The new Spode," she indicated the cups from which we were drinking, "I bought in a shop in the Bahamas. Almost everything else, however, came from auctions."

Like the study, the remainder of the house is full of individually appealing yet entirely complementary furniture and accessories. Was this decorative harmony the result of conscious choice, I wondered?

"Not in the sense that I sat down and made a list of what I wanted. You can't do that and buy at auctions; it would take forever. What I do try to do is to look at everything offered at auction in light of how I want the room in which it would logically go to look and how I want the room to perform for me."

That made sense, but it seemed that sticking to this process might be more difficult than this smiling woman made it sound. I asked her if she never made mistakes, never bought home something that she wanted to stick in a dark corner and forget.

"Of course, I do. Everyone who goes to auctions for any length of time makes some mistakes, but I really haven't bought too many things that I've later regretted. I think it's because I do look at everything to be sold very carefully before it goes on the block. I'm very cautious. Anything that I'm at all interested in, I make a note of in a looseleaf tablet that I carry with me to all sales. I also note approximately what I'm willing to pay for anything I've noted, so when the sale begins, I'm ready and I'm not tempted to bid on something that won't bear close inspection."

What if she doesn't get to the sale in time to look at the merchandise that closely?

"I rarely buy anything that I have not looked at ahead of time. If I do, it has to be so cheap that I don't mind throwing it away if it turns out to be something other than it seemed on the block."

What does she do with her mistakes?

"Well, I don't put them in dark corners, and I don't believe in accumulating a lot of odds and ends in the attic.

If what I no longer want is something nice, I use it as a Christmas or birthday gift for some friend who might enjoy it. Otherwise, I let a friend who has periodic garage sales dispose of it. I certainly wouldn't keep a mistake around; it's too depressing."

How many auctions has she attended during her lifetime?

"I couldn't begin to tell you, but it's been a rare week when I didn't go to at least one. My husband was just as big a buff as I."

How often does she buy?

"It depends. I've bought as many as ten items in one sale, and I've gone months without buying anything except a few novelty items for my grandchildren. I've reached the stage where I don't really need anything in the sense that I did when I was first collecting and had an empty house to fill. Now the only reason that I buy for myself is when something comes up that pleases me much more than something similar which I already possess. That gilt inkwell in the study, for instance, replaces one in majolica that I used for years. Since it had always been a favorite of my daughter's, I gave the majolica inkwell to her when I bought the one I have now."

As we talked, I became increasingly aware of the quality of her purchases. Had a dealer or decorator helped her buy?

"Oh no. For one thing, I've never really had very much money to spend. All of my auctiongoing has been done on a strict budget, and the buying commission that I would have had to pay a dealer would have meant that much less money to spend. Too, what's the fun of it if someone else does it for you? Whatever its merits or defects, this is my house—not someone else's idea of what it should be. Besides, my husband was remarkably good at spotting exceptional pieces, and he was always very interested in the house and how it looked. It always helps when there's someone close to you who enjoys talking about the sale and what you should buy and why."

Since she had formed the collection without professional aid, I asked her how she gained the knowledge so evident in what she had assembled over the years. Had she, I wondered, embarked on a serious course of study?

"Not really, although that probably would have been helpful. Still, when you're beginning a collection, you've no idea how much you don't know. I suppose you might say I soaked up what I know. A little from books and magazines, a little from going around and looking at museums and at merchandise in shops. And a lot from going to auctions themselves. If you go around long enough, it's hard not to learn."

Was the learning process the reason she attended even auctions where there was little likelihood that she would buy?

"Partially, but mostly I just enjoy auctions. Some people play bridge; I go to auctions. There's a lot of drama in the most ordinary auction if you just open your eyes to see it. And the merchandise never ceases to fascinate me. Even though I wouldn't dream of buying most of it, I like to watch the variety. It's always surprising to see what people will buy and what they will pay for it."

This led me to ask her what she thought of the new antiques.

"I suppose you mean those dreadful claw-footed oak tables and the rusty advertising signs and those funny little 1930s souvenir ash trays from Ramsgate? I'm afraid that I'm prejudiced. They may be new, but they're not what I would call antiques. Even ten years ago most of them would have bought almost nothing but a few laughs if it even occurred to anyone to put them up for sale. Now I see more and more of them coming up and getting good prices. I know that many young people actually prefer them."

She sighed. "I wouldn't be comfortable with most of the new antiques, but then I'm sure they mean something quite different to another generation. If they're what young people want, I certainly see nothing wrong in them. I might as well not."

She sat silently for a moment, looking at her own preferences, then laughed rather abruptly. "I've had it put in my will that my things are to be sold at auction, you know. I thought it only appropriate since that's how we got so many of them in the first place. Also, I've seen too many of my friends try to saddle their children with possessions not of their choosing. It rarely works. Either one has an emotional response to an object, or it's meaningless, no matter how fine the object may be. Just because a young man or a young woman is one's child is no guarantee that his or her emotional response will be the same as one's own. Possessions can be tyrannical, and I would not impose that tyranny on my children. This way my son and my daughter can bid on whatever they want and not have the rest of it forced on them so that they feel they must keep it."

"I've even toyed with the idea of liquidating my possessions myself. It would be fun in a way to be at the auction of one's own collection, but I find that I'm not able to face giving up all of the things that my husband and I found together. When the day comes, I just hope it's a good sale. It is, I think, one of the nicest things about auction that the things are sold to the people who really want them, and I'd like to think that my things will give other people the same joy that they've given me."

CASE HISTORY NO. 4
The Spasmodic Addicts

Diana and Paul M. are in their late twenties. They married two weeks after graduating from college. Diana is an actuarial clerk at a large life insurance company, Paul an instructor in math at a city college. They live on the fringes of an urban renewal area in a large Northern city and are still working on the renovation of the nineteenth-century house that they bought two years ago.

Like their house, their furnishings are incomplete. Some rooms still stand empty. "We're in no hurry," Diana explained. "We'd rather buy one thing a year and have it be the right thing than buy a lot of furniture just to fill up space." That they practice what they preach is immediately evident in their high-ceilinged living room.

Its startlingly white walls are hung with colorful posters. There are several prints of works by Aubrey Beardsley, framed in slashes of orange or purple. Over the mantel hangs an enormous canvas, a collage of nails and screws and alphabet block letters liberally coated with shiny mauve paint. Plain white shades hang at the long windows. For seating there are black and white deck chairs and oversized, furry acrylic pillows on the floor. A rug of straw matting lies over carefully refinished wood parquet. Dominating the room is an enormous Victorian sideboard of the Renaissance Revival period, crawling with fearsome creatures sculpted of walnut. On its shelves sits a collection of animals in different media, some strictly representational, some fanciful. The sideboard's black marble top supports candlesticks of every conceivable size and composition. The large base of the sideboard, concealed by beautifully veneered double doors, stores games in one side and a fully equipped bar in the other.

"That sideboard came from auction right after we got married. We got it for almost nothing. I'm not kidding," Paul insisted. "It was less than $30. Nobody wanted it because it was so big. It was a pain getting it here, but it was worth it."

"We call it our smoke screen," Diana laughed, "because with it in here nobody notices what else is or isn't in the room."

"Some of the animals on its shelves came from auctions too," Paul continued. "In fact, some of them cost more than the sideboard. At least half the candlesticks are auction finds. Everything else in this room we bought at department stores or received as gifts from friends."

"But our bed came from an auction," Diana interrupted. "It's really wild—brass curlicues you wouldn't believe. It wasn't as much of a buy as the sideboard, but it was still a lot less than it would have been in a good antique shop."

"Actually, there are things scattered through the whole house that came from one auction or another, like the old chopping block table in the kitchen and the wicker in the sun room. And we got a fairly new Amana refrigerator that has never given us any trouble for about a sixth of what it would have cost new," Paul said. "It's funny, but we rarely go to a sale without seeing something that we can use and enjoy."

Are they always able to buy it?

"Are you kidding? Sometimes people will run up the bid to a point where the price starts getting ridiculous. When that happens, we drop out. There has to be a limit somewhere."

"I think most of my favorite things have come from auctions," Diana mused. "It's funny too, because we don't go that much. When our friends ask us where this or that came from and we say 'an auction' they kid us about spending all our time at auctions. But we don't. I guess we don't go more than a dozen times a year, tops. But, as Paul said, we usually find something we like whenever we go. Too, we buy a lot of gifts at auction. We can get something a lot nicer for the same amount of money we'd spend retail."

When I asked why their attendance was so infrequent, they looked at each other and laughed. "It sounds silly," Paul began, "but we go in spurts."

"We won't go to an auction for months, then we'll go to every sale we can for two or three weeks," Diana said.

"It just works out that way," Paul added. "Usually we'll be in the mood to go somewhere one nice Saturday, and we'll read in the paper about an auction being held out in the country within easy driving distance. We pack a picnic lunch, and we go. Then we enjoy ourselves so much that we look to see if any more auctions are being held in our area during the next week. If there are and we can go, we do."

What signals the end of the spurt?

"Somebody outbids us on something we wanted very much," Diana explained.

"Or we get mad at something the auctioneer does, or all the merchandise is bad," Paul agreed.

"I guess it's when we hit one that isn't fun. It kills the mood, and we don't go again for awhile."

Don't they find it hard to keep up with prices and shifts in merchandise offerings by going that way?

"It doesn't really matter," Paul admitted. "We buy what we like and pay any price we can afford until it starts getting—as I said before—ridiculously high."

And they don't find that they lose their feel?

"Auctions are like dancing," Diana said firmly. "Once you start again, it's as if you'd never stopped."

CASE HISTORY NO. 5
The Non-Addict

Jack V. is a salesman for an estate planning firm. "They call us financial specialists, but basically we're salesmen," he explained. He advises people in middle to upper income brackets how to invest and spend their money to maximize tax advantages and opportunities for capital appreciation, his advice almost always including the importance of purchasing mutual funds and life insurance from his firm. It is a very high pressure job, and he admits the need to get away from business occasionally. He used to do this playing golf; now he goes to auctions.

"I still play golf, but it's strictly business to help convince a client to work with me. It doesn't relax me any more."

"Do auctions?" I asked.

"No way. I think auctions are the most frustrating thing in the world."

Then why go?

"I guess it's because I like to see the suckers get taken. Throwing away good money on all that junk. It's pretty funny, I can tell you."

Then he never buys anything?

"Only good stuff. I got this stuffed deer head in my den at an auction. That black iron doorstop—the one shaped like a ship—came from an auction, and so did this table." He pointed to a whitewashed table made from bits of tree limbs wired together and topped with a piece of board bound in rattan.

"But most auctions are a gyp from the word go. If the stuff was any good, it wouldn't be up for auction anyway. Somebody in the family would want it."

Looking around his pleasantly furnished home in this affluent suburb, I wondered how his wife felt about his hobby and the things that he bought.

"She thinks auctions are dirty. All that dust bothers her sinus, she says. So I go alone, or sometimes my oldest boy Jackie goes with me. He's 14, and he seems to like going pretty well. About what I buy—well, she says she doesn't care as long as I don't try to put it in the living room."

When did he start auctiongoing?

"Oh, it must have been five years ago, I guess. I had some papers for a client to sign, and he was going out of town the next day. He asked if I could meet him at this auction gallery, the same one I usually go to now, so he could look them over. I went and stayed. I thought it was one of the funniest things I'd ever seen. He was a funny sort of guy, the client, I mean."

How often does he go now?

"The house I like has sales every week. I try to go to at least two a month. With my work load, that's about all I can manage."

But why go so often just to watch people doing something that seems foolish to him?

"Oh, they're not all dumb," he protested. "You ought to watch some of those men sometimes, the women too. They've got the auctioneer's number all right. Some of those people really know that they're doing. It's the cuckoos who tickle me. Some of the things they'll buy!"

When I tactfully pointed out that tastes differ and that it was possible that his stuffed deer head, magnificent though it might be, could strike someone else as superfluous to the requirements of modern life, he surprisingly agreed.

"That's so. People do like different things, but some of that stuff that some of those oddballs buy nobody would want, at least nobody in their right mind.

"I suppose what I really like about auctions is that sometimes things do come up that you never see in the stores. Maybe it's just something that you've always wanted—like that deer head—or maybe it's something that looks like something that was in your grandma's house—like the table, but it's *different* from the kind of merchandise that you can walk into a store and buy. I don't see buying things at auction that you can buy new. I'd rather have the new."

But does he find auctions fun?

"Yes, I suppose I do," he said thoughtfully. "But I still can't understand those people who really get hooked. It's just something to do, that's all."

Chapter 12

Wrapping It Up

A country auction operator said to me a few months ago, "Who's making the money? I'm not. The haulers aren't. The dealers say they're not. Who is?" One auctiongoer after another insisted that he or she certainly was not benefitting, that auction prices seemed to be increasing as rapidly as overall quality of merchandise declined.

In spite of this widespread sense of dissatisfaction on both sides of the block, however, auctions thrive in this country, perhaps as never before. The number of houses proliferates nationwide; the auctioneering schools graduate bumper crops of enthusiastic beginners; would-be consignors seem less suspicious of the process; and the number of auctiongoers steadily increases.

In this book I have attempted to give you a sense of this

activity and to put forth certain observations of my own about the process and how to use it to your advantage. It is inevitable that your own experience with auctions may prompt you to disagree with me—perhaps violently. About any operation as complex and diversified as the auction, there are bound to be differences of opinion; and this is good because it prompts the auctiongoer to think about what he is doing at auction and why. At best, this book has given you a skeleton, possibly an incomplete one at that; only the sheer fun of auctions can clothe it with flesh.

I think of the first auction that I attended, a little country sale in a town a few miles north of here. The haulers who stocked it were probably some of the most inconsistent of their breed. They would present a dozen cases of reproduction Mason jars with as much aplomb as they would an Empire game table, and their loads were likely to include anything.

A prefabricated metal building, one of those that looks like a corrugated, elongated child's building block, was the hall, so arranged and ventilated that one froze in winter and fried in summer. The auctioneer was straight from Actor's Equity. He called bids with a cigar clamped between his teeth; and he was not above occasionally snapping the black arm bands that he wore over his spotlessly white shirt, just above the elbow on each arm. His floor man was a natural comic—faintly loopy grin, bovine eyes, short stocky build, and a bald head that glistened with sweat in the bright lights.

The floor man loved plates. They were his meat and champagne. No matter their quality, condition, or provenance—all were treated alike. He'd pick one up, glance quickly at its front, then flip it over. If it had no mark, he'd hold it up high and yell, "Let's sell this purty piece." But if there were a mark, he would peer at it from every angle, then intone reverentially, "It's an old one. Got markings on the back."

As might be expected in any assembly where Chanel No. 5 contended with but was usually defeated by a thick aura of sweat and stale cigar smoke, the audience was a mixed bag. Farmers from the surrounding countryside would

come in to bid on the manure spreaders, plows, and other old hand tools that regularly started every sale. (From their comments, most of these anachronistic implements—this was before rising gasoline costs— were destined to become mailbox holders, in what way I hadn't the nerve to ask.) Many young families from the town furnished their first homes from this auction hall with turn-of-the-century oak. Operators of the "Ye Olde Spinning Wheele" type antique shops lining the highways out of town contested bitterly for anything primitive or with the potential of becoming primitive. A few affluent types from the city snapped up the better quality, older items that occasionally turned up and invariably sold for bargain prices.

It was a volatile mix. On nights when prices were going

high, the regulars would begin to mutter nastily about halfway through the sale. The word would then be passed: the haulers themselves must be bidding up the prices.

The two haulers, who looked as if they might have interrupted successful wrestling careers to take up their present profession, always stood to one side of the heaped merchandise. They never looked happy. I can't remember seeing either of them smile. Their normal expression was that of bored disgust. On nights when the muttering from the audience was especially obvious and it became clear that some auctiongoers were going to protest by refusing to bid on anything, the disgust would give way to confused rage. Then the haulers would stand, all but exploding from their tight flannel shirts and jeans and growl. Upon occasion the smaller and scrappier of the two would decide that he at any rate had had enough.

"If you blank, blank people think we've hauled this blank, blank junk this far to *give* it to you, you're blank, blank out of your blank, blank heads." Just as his face would reach a shade of crimson of which Parker's ink would be proud, the operator of the auction—who was even larger than the haulers—would remove him bodily from the premises, in the process nearly garroting him with the collar of his red flannel shirt.

All muttering would stop, and the auction would continue as if nothing had happened. Prices, however, would tend to be lower.

At most auctions, bidders tend to be mutually tolerant of one another's selections, fearful no doubt of jocularity directed at their own. No such reluctance inhibited this crowd. It was a rare item that failed to elicit at least one derisory hoot. Women in wedgies and Lane Bryant cable knits—fresh from their triumphs in "stealing" for seventy-five cents apiece fruit jars that could be bought for two dollars a dozen in the five and dime—would go into hysterics at other dealers willing to risk five dollars for a box of books.

We never learned what happened to that auction. We were out of town for a few weeks; and when we came back, it was out of business. The careless piles of dusty furniture and mildewed books had been replaced by neat stacks of appliance parts.

It had been, in many ways, a mediocre sale even on its better nights, yet in the few months between our discovery of it and its premature demise, we bought half a dozen unusual items of good quality that have brought us much pleasure and remain among our favorite possessions. The merchandise cost us less than $100; the memories were free.

Since then we have learned that almost every auction shares one thing with that long gone sale: a personality of its own. And it is that personality which makes the memories. It may be more sane and sanitary to shop at Macy's, but the auction is a lot more fun.

Useful Terms

Advance—the increment by which the bid continues; may be as small as 25c on inexpensive items and as high as $5,000 on a valuable lot.

All or choice—a multi-piece lot of which the successful bidder can buy one or several items at a price per item equal to the amount of the successful bid.

As is—the article as you see it, with the house accepting no responsibility for chips, cracks, tears, or other existing imperfections.

Auctioneer—the man or woman conducting the sale.

Bid—price offered.

Book-bid—bid left with auctioneer in advance of sale.

Buyer's privilege—the opportunity given a successful bidder on first of several identical lots to buy the remaining lots at the same price before they go on the block.

Choice—see "All or choice."

Consignor—the person or organization owning or controlling the merchandise on the block.

Consignment—auction merchandise not owned or controlled by the house.

Estimate—the price the house tells the consignor to expect to receive on an item; in effect, an informal appraisal of current market value.

Floor man—the person who directs the movement and

handling of merchandise during the sale; also may help spot bids.

Helpers—the people who handle the merchandise during the sale.

House—the establishment offering the sale.

Knocked-down—sold.

Lot—the unit offered for sale; may be one article or several.

Pass—decision made by auctioneer to skip a lot.

Planting—practice of inserting unlike or inferior articles in a lot.

Price—the amount for which an item is sold.

Provenance—the ownership and exhibition history of an item.

Reserve—the minimum price the consignor will accept for an article, sometimes silent, sometimes stated by the auctioneer.

Shill—a house employee posing as a member of the audience to run up the bidding.

Sponsor—the organization under whose auspices a benefit sale is held.

Unrestricted sale—an auction in which there are no minimums, or reserves and all merchandise is to be sold to the highest bidder.

Index